Innovation

£10

Also available in this Series

Management and Marketing Series

Innovation in Marketing

New Perspectives for Profit and Growth

THEODORE LEVITT

**Professor of Business Administration,
Harvard University Graduate School of
Business Administration**

UNABRIDGED

PAN BOOKS LTD : LONDON

First published 1962 by McGraw-Hill, Inc.
This edition published in UK 1968 by Pan Books Ltd.,
33 Tothill Street, London, S.W.1

330 02177 X

*Printed in Great Britain
by Richard Clay (The Chaucer Press), Ltd.,
Bungay, Suffolk*

PREFACE

THIS BOOK is about marketing, but in the broadly encompassing sense, not in the narrow functional sense. It conceives of marketing not as a business function but as a profit-building view of the entire business process.

The book clearly distinguishes between selling and marketing, and suggests that a strictly sales-oriented approach to doing business can be suicidal. The difference between selling and marketing is more than semantic. Selling focuses on the needs of the seller, marketing on the needs of the buyer. Selling is preoccupied with the seller's need to convert his product or service into cash; marketing with the idea of satisfying the needs of the customer by means of the product or service and by the whole cluster of customer-getting value satisfactions associated with creating, delivering, and finally consuming it.

But that is only part of the story, and besides it is merely a theoretical statement. What counts in the end is its successful execution in practical cases. One purpose of this book is to show how specifically to convert the theoretical statement into concrete results. This foreword cannot do that.

A book's foreword is often the disillusioning place where the author suddenly discovers that he can say in a few pithy paragraphs what he has so ponderously said in the several hundred pages that follow. It can be an afterthought that gets into the reader's way of doing what he has paid good money to do – namely, read the book.

My intention here is to clear the way, not get into it. My only other substantive comment therefore is that this book is addressed to the busy, able, and responsible men who constantly look for ways of improving their difficult jobs of managing the complex and exciting affairs of business in this fast-moving age.

But for the details the reader will have to see for himself. He will have to get on with a very simple and necessary job. He will have to read the book, cover to cover.

In the meantime, I want to mention some of the people whose influence has helped shape this book. There is Valdemar Carlson of Antioch College, who got me into the college that I owe so much and whose vigorous blue pencil years ago was an especially effective literary disciplinarian; the late Lewis Corey, who fanned my interest in technology and demonstrated that a vigorous social critic can also be a vigorous defender and admirer of what he criticizes; H. Gordon Hayes of New Orleans, who set an inspiring example of intellectual youthfulness and tough-minded literary simplicity; Arthur Salz of Columbus, Ohio, whose painstakingly prepared and deceptively quiet lectures were in reality like Austerlitz battles and whose intellectual style was like a Promethean fire; S. Morris Livingston of Chicago, who got me into and methodically taught me the oil business; Robert C. Gunness of the Standard Oil Co. (Indiana), who had the foresight and fortitude to sponsor new ideas and break new ground; F. Cushing Smith of the American Oil Company, whose patience and encouragement provided a usefully protective haven for exploring new approaches to old problems; Vernon A. Bellman, Baxter F. Ball, G. A. Klaffky, Harry J. Peckheiser, and J. B. Merrell of the Mobil Oil Company, who encouraged and supported new ideas in marketing organization and planning; Edward C. Bursk and Edmund P. Learned of the Harvard Business School, who helped bring me to the School which has provided the stimulation, learning, and time which helped produce this book; and my wife, Joan, who provides the numerous personal satisfactions without which few other things are worth doing. Finally, I want to acknowledge a profound debt to my father, Boris Levitt, for his modestly projected example of the satisfying virtues of hard work, personal dignity, responsibility, self-discipline, pride in craftsmanship, and continuing social awareness.

Theodore Levitt

SOURCES

SOME CHAPTERS of this book are partly based on materials previously published elsewhere by the author. Credit should be given to the following sources of portions of the indicated chapters.

CHAPTER 3: 'Marketing Myopia', *Harvard Business Review*, July–August 1960.

CHAPTER 5: 'Growth and Profit through Planned Marketing Innovation', *Journal of Marketing*, April 1960.

CHAPTER 6: 'Thinking Ahead about the Business Future', in *Effective Marketing Action*, edited by David W. Ewing, Harper & Brothers, 1958.

CHAPTER 7: 'Blue-skies Approach to Tomorrow's Marketing', *Business Horizons*, Spring, 1958.

CHAPTER 9: 'Management versus the Failure of Commercial Research', *Advanced Management*, October 1959.

CHAPTER 10: 'M-R Snake Dance', *Harvard Business Review*, November–December 1960.

CONTENTS

1

CUSTOMERS AND BUSINESSMEN

THE PRIMARY business of every business is to stay in business. And to do that you have to get and keep customers. This is usually interpreted to mean that you have to sell what you have.

One of the central themes of this book is that this just isn't so. Things are both simpler and more complex than that.

Every statement addresses itself to a customer. This book certainly does. This is also true of the minister addressing his Sunday flock, the politician proposing a programme, and even the 'far-out' abstract painter who resolutely proclaims his non-conformist hostility to the world. No matter how much the painter professes his independence from society by asserting his devotion to 'art for art's sake', he still paints with the hope of attracting the solicitous attention of some anonymous but solvent admirer.

It may be reducing things to callous simplicity to say so, but the fact is that everybody is selling something the minute he opens his mouth – whether he lives in a capitalist society, a communist society, or in some exotic utopia. But some people sell professionally. It is their life, their bread and butter. A capitalist society such as ours has a lot of professional sellers. Without them we wouldn't be capitalist, and some people say persuasively that we wouldn't be free either.

Selling is as basic to our society as metabolism is to life. It might be argued that selling *is* the metabolism of free enterprise. And since our society is thoroughly committed to the system of free enterprise, one would naturally expect that its people are thoroughly committed to the idea of selling – that they openly accept the crucial role of selling and salesmanship, and that salesmen are honoured citizens. It is the salesmen who keep the system in healthful good shape. The wheels of industry are made to hum, income is generated, standards of living are raised, and in the process even leisure time is generated during which people can indulge such higher tastes as reading T. S. Eliot and going to the opera.

But, curiously, selling just doesn't have this lofty status in America. In fact, it occupies one of the lowest rungs on the occupational status ladder. A careful study of occupational prestige ratings conducted jointly by the National Opinion Research Center and the Graduate School of Ohio State University a few years ago showed that Americans rank salesmen far below airline pilots, electricians, biologists, radio announcers, civil engineers, public-school instructors, railroad engineers, and machinists.

It would be reassuring to attribute this dismal performance to ignorance. It would be even more reassuring to attribute it to the corrosive propaganda of communists and malcontents. But this was a careful and scientific sampling of the entire spectrum of our population.

The lowly rating of sales and selling in American society is reflected in the way these words are used in the American language. Even such an incorruptibly objective authority as *Webster's New International Dictionary* sounds a sour note. A good dictionary tells many things, not just how to spell a word and what it means. In giving a definition, it also reflects the society's attitudes about the meaning of the word. Here is the full transcript on the word 'sell' from *Webster's New Collegiate Dictionary*:

sell (sel), *v.t.*; SOLD (sold); SELL′ING. [AS. *sellan, syllan*, to give, deliver, sell.] 1. To deliver or hand over in breach of duty, trust, etc.; to betray. 2. To deliver into bondage, esp. for money. 3. To dispose of or manage for profit instead of in accord with conscience, justice, etc.; as, to *sell* one's vote. 4. *Slang.* To impose upon; trick. 5. To transfer (property) for a consideration; to give up for a consideration; to convey; – opposed to buy. 6. To deal in as an article of sale; as, to *sell* groceries – *v.i.* 1. To dispose of commodities or property; to make sales. 2. To be sold; to find buyers. – sell out. 1. To dispose of completely by sale. 2. *Slang*. To betray one's cause or associates for a compensation. 3. *Exchanges*. To sell in open market (stocks or commodities carried on margin when this margin is not maintained); also, to sell the stocks or commodities of (a person) in this way and for this reason. – *n. Colloq.* A hoax.[1]

For a country as firmly committed to the capitalist way of life as ours, this suspicious and hostile attitude towards selling and salesmen seems odd indeed. As the above transcript confirms again, our attitude towards selling is strong, unambiguous, and unflattering. We think of it as unworthy and base. Yet selling is something every business does. The lives of all of us depend inexorably on commerce, of which selling is a vital part.

All of us constantly sell something, even if only our skills and personalities. We sell eagerly, but we buy suspiciously. As customers, our first reaction to a sales situation is fear: Are we being 'sold a bill of goods'? The word 'sell' serves as a description of the worst offence a man can commit against his country: 'The traitor, he sold out to the enemy.' The greatest deceit a man can commit against a trusting friend is described in terms of 'sell': 'He sold him down the river.' Even salesmen don't like to refer to their selling activities. All kinds of euphemisms have been invented to avoid calling a salesman a 'salesman'. Companies officially call their salesmen 'account executives', 'product representatives', and 'sales engineers'. In a manner of apologetic jest a salesman at a non-business cocktail party is apt to describe himself to a stranger as a 'pedlar'. This, however, is really a calculated tactic designed both to disarm and to befriend his new acquaintance. When the salesman tells his listener that he is a pedlar, he intends to say, in effect, that he himself doesn't think much of his own occupation. In this way presumably he hopes to tell the listener that

[1] By permission. From *Webster's New Collegiate Dictionary*, copyright 1961 by G. & C. Merriam Co, Publishers of the Merriam-Webster Dictionaries.

in spite of his profession, he's a decent guy. Thus the new acquaintance is presumably put into the position of saying to himself, 'He seems to be a nice sort of fellow, even if he is a salesman.' At the same time the 'pedlar' comment relieves the listener of the chore of having to make some pleasant comment about 'salesmen', a group of people of whom he is assumed not to be particularly fond.

In a nation where buying is so popular, why is selling so unpopular? You can't have buying without selling, yet people who enjoy buying don't enjoy sellers. Certainly the distaste and distrust of selling and salesmen are not things that were bred into primeval man on the original day of creation. He has learned them somewhere.

Chances are his opinion is based on costly experience. He *has* been sold a bill of goods. Long before capitalism was invented, Eve sold Adam a bill of goods for which we are still supposed to be paying. As the result of this shady deal, we are committed to a life in which 'By the sweat of thy brow shalt thou eat bread'. The Romans, who had the right and ringing phrase for everything, tried to alert the buyer to his peril with the declaration, *caveat emptor*, or, 'let the buyer beware'. Of whom? The seller, of course. Even Adam Smith, the paternal and sympathetic philosopher of capitalist economic theory, declared that 'The interest of the dealers . . . is always in some respects different from, and even opposite to, that of the public'.

The reason selling is a dirty word is because in the experience of a lot of people selling is a dirty business. This is not so because it is inherently dirty or because people have been done some deliberate dirt, but because there is a natural and irremovable difference of interests between sellers and buyers. I do not say that there is a natural conflict of interests, but there is a natural difference. For one thing, the seller usually knows more about the defects or limitations of a product or a service than the buyer. The seller is an expert, the buyer at best only a well-informed amateur. When the buyer is unsatisfied or is let down by what he finally takes home he is justified in assuming that the seller deliberately withheld some of the facts. One such experience is enough to sour any man on salesmen. Even salesmen have become soured on salesmen for precisely this kind of reason.

Occurrences of this kind may be rare, but a man's hard-earned cash is a dear commodity. He can hardly be criticized for slightly exaggerating the extent of the duplicity by which he was so smoothly and, he thinks, larcenously separated from his cherished cash.

Out-and-out larceny is rare these days. At least it is rare compared to the abundance of sales honesty and satisfied customers. Moreover, a lot of what passes for larceny or being sold a bill of goods or even not getting exactly what you hoped for – a lot of this is as inevitable and inescapable as buying and selling themselves. The buyer understandably wants something close to total perfection. The seller can seldom know everything the buyer really requires, and even less of what he really wants. If he buys a suit of clothes he wants not just decent clothing but also a fashion suitable to his particular style of life, a colour that fits a particular gap in his wardrobe, a cut that wows the ladies or pleases his wife, and a fit that hides his paunch, or accentuates his masculinity, or evens up his drooping left shoulder. The seller can't know all these things because the buyer is seldom aware of them all himself, even though they later become factors in his irritation at the salesman for not having given him what he *really* wanted.

The same sort of complex calculation goes into the irritation of the plant manager at not having got exactly what he wanted when he bought a new conveyor system and into that of the corporation president at not having got exactly what he wanted from the expensive consultants who reorganized his staff operation.

The buyer's dissatisfaction with the seller is an inescapable fact of life. His suspicion of the salesman is as natural as his need for sleep. Hence it makes no more sense for salesmen and associations of salesmen to go about the country proclaiming their sterling virtues and preaching against the attacks of a hostile public than it makes sense to complain about the absence of water on the desert. That's what a desert is – a place without water. That's what the seller–buyer relationship is – a transaction in which each side gets something he wants that the other side has, but where the buyer is usually left with a residual of discontent. That's life.

But that does not mean the situation can't be improved, any more than that you can't get water in the desert. If you dig deeply enough you will get water. In the selling-buying situation, if the seller digs deeply enough to discover the real needs and wants of the buyer, he can reduce this residual of discontent by raising the positive element of clear-cut satisfaction. In the process the seller will also sell more, keep more customers, and, above all, create and get more customers.

The idea and process of doing this kind of digging, and the action which follows it, are called 'marketing'. It is not selling. In fact, marketing is as different from selling as chemistry is from alchemy, astronomy from astrology, chess from checkers.

The object of this book is, first of all, to show the inescapable necessity of top management's having a passionate marketing view of its job. The second object is to demonstrate what marketing really is, how it differs from selling, and how individuals and companies can successfully orient and organize themselves for bigger profits and foster growth. Essentially what this book does is to look at management basically as a marketing function, to look at marketing not as a business function but as a comprehensive view of the entire business process.

But it does not make the simple-minded suggestion that a business's prosperity hinges merely on everybody being a better salesman or on refining the subtle arts of separating the unwary consumer from his loose change. Rather, it stresses the profound importance of the business firm's organizing itself to take more effective care of the customer's constantly changing needs and values, and it shows how to do it.

This book is not a do-gooder treatise on how to be a better citizen by serving society better. It is intended as a tough-minded explanation, outline, and example of how to serve yourself better by serving the customer better.

Most businesses and most sellers now think they do a pretty good job of marketing, of discovering and taking care of the customer's complex needs. Large and small companies hire market-research specialists to find out what the customer wants, how to supply him better, and whether the present product or service is adequate. An orgiastic amount of time, money, and talent go into these operations. The sales department that goes strictly on hunch and flies exclusively by the seat of its pants is getting as rare as a prohibitionist.

But in spite of all the apparent eagerness for consumer information, it is not hard to show that this seldom produces any really solid advances in the creation of customer satisfaction, and hence none in sales or profits. Most such advances are still more the result of luck and pluck than of thorough-going wisdom. The trouble is not that the consumer isn't researched enough or that the men at the corporate top aren't smart enough to use the information wisely and creatively. It is that all too often neither the researchers nor the corporate bosses really know what it is they are trying to do.

Sure, they want to make money, to become important, to be secure, even to expand and grow. But the trouble, as I shall show later, is that they are trying to do it as sellers, not as marketers. They go through the respectable ritual of trying to find out what the customer needs and wants, but in the end they are more interested in how these facts can be used to lure the customer to the product than in how they can be used to modify the product and its delivery so that the customer will really prefer it over all its competitors.

This distinction may sound like an academic difference worthy only of an academic discussion. It may seem like splitting hairs. At worst, it may sound like namby-pamby nonsense. But before anybody gets too self-satisfied with his own feeling of practical virtue, let me point out that in business, as in love, war, and poker, it's the small differences in the beginning that make the big differences in the end.

For example, in love it was his slightly greater wisdom and tranquillity that legendarily won Cleopatra for Caesar, even though he was older and less dashing than the handsome Mark

Antony. In war, it was an extra increment of mobility that won the African campaign for Montgomery, even though Rommel had great cunning and more initiative. And in poker, nobody needs to be told how the slightest difference in cards or in the way the game is played makes the biggest difference in the outcome. Hopefully, reading this book will become the small difference that produces big profit-building differences for its readers.

2

CHANGE AND BUSINESS STRATEGY

ASSOCIATE SUPREME Court Justice Oliver Wendell Holmes once found himself on a train and unable to locate his ticket. While the conductor watched, he unsuccessfully foraged through all his pockets. Finally, the conductor recognized him and said, 'Mr Holmes, don't worry; you don't need the ticket. You'll probably find it after you get off the train, and I'm sure the Pennsylvania Railway Company will trust you to mail it back later.' The Justice looked up at him with some irritation and said, 'My dear man, that's not the problem at all. The problem is not, where is my ticket? The problem is, where am I going?'

If you don't know where you're going, any road will take you there. The main job of the chief executive is to know where his company is going. In a survey Dun & Bradstreet, Inc., took in 1960 of the presidents of the nation's 170 biggest corporations the largest single group of them said the best-managed companies are those that are strong on long-range planning, where the chief executives have put their main efforts into charting the future.

The answer to the question of where your company is and should be going depends on a lot of things. It depends on where the company has been, what its competence and strengths are, what the competition is doing, and what is happening out there in society and in the consumer's enigmatic mind.

One thing we know for sure about society and consumers is that they are constantly changing in ways that are extremely important to every business. The trick is to anticipate and act on these changes before the competition does, and to do it at the right time and in the right way.

We live in a world of galloping change. Everybody knows it and is told the story repeatedly. But we have always lived in a world of change – it is the history of the world. Still, there is a unique quality to the changes which assault us these days: they come faster than ever before; they are less predictable; they are more encompassing in their impact; and they are more varied in their nature.

All this creates new problems and opportunities for every executive. The new forces that are so continuously and implacably arrayed against us make each of us constantly modify traditional ways of thinking and doing things. One tradition that is being rapidly altered is the definition of the job of management itself, particularly top management. Top management is getting to be more marketing-oriented, more concerned with the booming, buzzing conditions of the external world to which the firm ultimately addresses itself. The previous major preoccupations of top management – financial and production problems and often legal affairs – are yielding to a new preoccupation with what are essentially marketing considerations. In Dun and Bradstreet's 1960 survey the 170 presidents ranked marketing competence first in accounting for the success of America's best-managed companies. Next in order came organizational planning, then research and development, then production techniques, then personnel management, then labour relations, and finally public relations. No wonder an official of the American Management Association told a 1959 AMA conference, perhaps with some exaggeration, that 'every company president elected from 1965 on will be a marketing man'. There is a new synthesis of what management does and should do – a sort of miscegenation of the traditional pigeonhole executive functions.

It is precisely because of the rapid pace of change in the world that marketing has become so pre-eminent. The reason is obvious: marketing is uniquely on the firing line where the impact of change is greatest for the business firm. Marketing is where the customer is, and it is the customer who in the end decides the fate of a business.

The most obvious types of changes that disrupt our lives

and make competitive existence more turbulent are the technological changes that bombard us these days in such cumulative abundance. Most of us are actually pretty ignorant about them. We know about the big glamorous ones like satellite TV projection, digital computers, automation, and perhaps high-frequency ultrasonic drilling and cleaning. But we know precious little about other changes that promise to alter our lives – things like negative-ion machines, which may greatly change our dietary habits and our work productivity in the next quarter of a century. These machines produce atmospheric electric charges that deeply affect people's metabolism and psychological attitudes. Negative ions are discharged in massive abundance before and during thunderstorms. It is these ions that make us all feel so exhilarated, fresh, and high-spirited during such storms. One day they will be in office and plant air-conditioning systems, automatically making 'better' men of us. Indeed, the machines are already on the market, including desk-sized ones for the individual worker. If you were in, say, the food-processing business this would certainly interest you. What will happen to your business when, all over the country in offices, factories, schools, and homes, these machines are silently ticking off this exhilarating sense of well-being and therefore lowering people's desire for, say, that mid-afternoon snack or coffee break which accounts for a substantial per cent of your annual sales?

Many of the changes which we see and which change our lives and the business environment are produced by the rampant pace of technology. But many changes, instead of being produced by technology, produce the technology itself. War, for example, produced the energy revolution that gave us the atomic bomb and jet and space travel. War also created the powerful new management tool of operations research – a tool that may make many of the management functions we perform today obsolete tomorrow. It also produced, in part, the population upheaval we all know about, and which in turn is setting off cumulative chains of events.

The inability or refusal of companies to see the opportunities produced by change often seems to be a peculiar affliction of big, well-organized companies. General Electric turned down the opportunity to get exclusive American rights to manufacture and distribute neon lights, saying there was no market for them. A new small company had to be organized by Europeans in the United States to pioneer this big, profitable market. Frozen orange juice had to be started by a company not in the food business. The big hotel chains fought the motel idea for years, in spite of its greater customer-satisfying benefits. The big vacuum-tube manufacturers (with the exception of Philco) vigorously resisted the transistor idea. The oxygenation process of greatly expanding the capacity of existing steel mills was well established in Sweden for a decade before it was first adopted in the United States, and then it was one of the smaller steel companies that did so.

Why do big companies so often seem to resist some of these changes so vigorously, acting only after the ideas are proved out, even when these companies pridefully promote their impressive slogans of progressiveness? Why is this complacency, this fat-cat constipation, so often a big-company problem? What can be done to avoid it?

The obvious way to avoid it is to become more systematically and sensitively aware of the changing characteristics of the world we live in – not just technological change but all the other forces that so ineluctably affect our affairs.

If business is something more than the mere issuing of things of predictable content, then it cannot be done in a bustle. The businessman must also be in the swim. His senses must be active on the social scene, and he must keep his discrimination focused upon something more than his own ruminations. Some firms exist in a sealed continuum, and so do their executives. This makes discrimination difficult, which in turn leads to the systematic rejection of new ideas in favour of the respectable virtues of the here and now. The law of nature which makes most men waste in spirit as they advance in years takes its dismal toll.

To accept new insights and to put across new ideas it is necessary not only to appreciate them but also to get excited about them. And this is impossible unless you understand reasonably well the changing characteristics of the society in which these insights and ideas are to be applied.

While technology, new products, and war produce change, so do social and political upheaval, people's values and tastes, their ways of living, working conditions, and family living habits. A look at a few of these areas will help to illustrate what they mean for various industries. It will show how, by examining them more carefully, executives can make themselves more sensitive to the strategic importance of some neglected aspects of change and therefore become better able to fit the significance of these changes into their daily thinking.

Product Changes. Probably the most significant product development of the twentieth century is the internal-combustion engine. Its obvious results are the car, the aeroplane, and everything that has so abundantly followed on their encompassing wake. It changed the structure of cities around the world, the location of industry, the occupational structure of the labour force, and certainly the courting and nuptial habits of young people. It has changed the nature of war, the clothes we wear, the structure and solidarity of the family. If your business has operations abroad, or is thinking in terms of foreign markets, what will the expanding use of the automobile do in countries where it isn't yet so widely owned? What can you do today to capitalize on the consequent changes that these countries will certainly undergo?

Television in the United States has also produced some powerful changes. It has, for example, increased the demand for cars among teen-agers. For them, the entry of the TV set into the living room has meant the decline of teen-age courting privacy. As a result, the car has become more than ever a sort of mobile parlour. And TV has affected eating habits – TV dinners and snack titbits. It has reduced the amount of evening pleasure driving and to this extent reduced gasoline consumption. In housing, TV has raised the demand for wall panelling. TV manufacturers pioneered the substitution of moulded plastics for steel in the housings of large pieces of equipment, thus showing producers of other products that they are less dependent on steel than they thought.

As an executive, did you personally, back in 1948, ever think about what impact TV might have on society and what business opportunities and problems it might create in your particular industry? Did you ask yourself this question: 'TV may produce a fundamental upheaval in our society. If so, what will be the significance for my business?' This is the sort of question the progressive business executive must constantly ask himself about the many changes that are constantly taking place. If he waits until the upheaval has already come, he is no better an observer than the mundane man on the street. And his company will be no more distinguished than that anonymous creature.

People's Values and Attitudes. People's values and attitudes on a variety of subjects can produce sudden and often enormous changes and opportunities. Continuing with the example of the food industry, for some years now we have had the cholesterol scare. People have been dieting almost compulsively. Actually there is a question of whether they diet because of cholesterol or because of sex. A good argument can be made for the latter. Our society has become enormously sex-oriented, not just in the United States but in Western Europe too. We see it in the many copulatory best sellers, in movies, in ads, in popular songs, and in fashions – especially now in men's fashions. For some years men's fashions have been emphasizing the slim, youthful look, with tight-fitting non-pleated pants. Movies all over the world seem to recognize the growing preoccupation of men with physical attractiveness – their Walter Mitty dreams of sexual prowess. And this is not just a fantasy of virile young men. It is a much more commonplace preoccupation of the mature middle-aged man. Anybody who cares to can get reliable evidence of this from the sudden mushrooming of articles on the subject in such scholarly publications as *The American Journal of Sociology*. But there is an even more handy source of evidence – the movies. It is significant that there has been a spate of movies showing ageing lotharios like Cary Grant, Vittorio de Sica, and the late Clark Gable majestically sweeping luscious young blondes off their well-shaped feet. Why are so many of the celluloid romantic heroes greying at the temples, while their willing paramours are youthful chicks? It can't just be accident or a shortage of young leading men. Something much more profound is going on.

The fact is that featuring these superannuated Don Juans capitalizes on the middle-aged man's new self-consciousness of his continuing masculinity. The middle-aged man today wants to believe that he still has a good fighting chance for an occasional exotic conquest, that he is indeed as young as he feels, and he feels great. Beyond that, the whole arrangement of ageing leading men paired with youthful ladies does something for that great mass of movie goers, teen-aged boys and girls. It is a school of adult love technique for the boys, and for the girls it suggests that their early years are no barrier to their quickly escaping the conventional sex limitations of extreme youth and moving rapidly into the world of adult perquisites.

These movies are a powerful reflection of the fact that today we all compulsively want to look and be young – and basically for sex reasons, whether we are aware of our complex motives or not. Faust's tragic wish to relive his virile youth just one more brief time describes the pervading psychological condition of the middle-aged urban man in all the developed countries of the Western world. While in the past middle-aged man kept his secret wishes buried deeply in private fantasies, today he lets them out and goes halfway along Faust's troubled trail.

He does it in part by dieting and by sartorial fastidiousness. The same is true in part for older women. They feel forced to remodel themselves into grotesque apparitions of attractive youthfulness, if only to keep their restless husbands from stealthily roving after more gamey prey. Look at the excessive lengths to which ageing matrons go to look youthful beyond their ability to carry off the deception. An obscure cosmetics company only a few years ago recognized this desire as a profit opportunity and began very effectively to promote its hair dyes. Now both the company and the industry are giants. For a man today to have greying temples is a sign of distinction and mature virility; for a woman it is a sign of criminal neglect.

But does this preoccupation with slimness and youthfulness hold any opportunities or pitfalls for your business? Let us say again that you are in the food-processing business. Without warning you see Mead Johnson Company, which is not in the food business, launching Metrecal – a runaway success. Why was it so successful? Was it because of the nation's new concern with heart disease or with physical attractiveness? Perhaps it makes no difference. The fact is that Mead Johnson is now your competitor, even if it is not in the food business. You might say that it is now in the 'not-food' or 'anti-food' business.

Metrecal, unlike television, is an example of a product being not the *cause* but the *result* of changing public habits, tastes, and values. But if you were in the food business, does the success of Metrecal and its imitators suggest that you are now in trouble – that people consume less conventional food – or does it mean that there might be opportunities for you? There are lots of ways of looking at this problem, such as shifting the emphasis of your various products' characteristics and of your line of products away from calories. But there are other, more subtle ways of looking at this matter which demonstrate how an executive who has trained himself to be thoroughly sensitive to change and customer needs might think and act.[1]

---

[1] Executives, probably more than any other single group, with the exception of young women, should long ago have been aware of the conditions that have produced the Metrecal craze. The nation's larger corporations have house doctors to proselyte the message of slim fitness. Magazines oriented towards businessmen feel themselves somehow negligent if they don't run an annual article on the importance of a sound and slimming diet.

Hence, more than most people, executives should have been aware years ago of this diet-happy, cholesterol-crazy condition of American life. But how many of them seriously stopped to raise the question of what problems or opportunities this might create for their businesses? Even companies that are not in any way in the food business should have asked themselves this. It affects steel companies, for example, because it affects the consumption of thin sheets used for canning food. And in view of the unrestrained way

You might say something like this to yourself: Lots of people are stooping to 900 calories in a day. They get some important psychological benefits besides the physical ones they are directly after. But, basically, sipping lunch through a straw is full of emptiness. It violates the ingrained idea that if you can't chew it it can't be very nourishing. It's unnatural. Something must be missing. Hence Metrecal maniacs will probably always wonder if they're not losing something in the form of energy and vitality, even though the ads tell them everything is rosy. Certainly these people would be easily suggestible to such an idea, as is evidenced by the booming sales of vitamins. People feel there is something missing in their diets, even though their diets are better now than they have ever been in the entire history of man. Yet to tell them that diets and Metrecal are energy-robbing, with the hope of their returning to more solid foods, would be a poor strategy, since they have a deep psychological and sex need to be slimly attractive. Hence, for you in the food business the obvious question is this: Since we can't fight the Metrecal idea, what can we do to join it?

You could imitate. But the market is already flooded with imitators. How about building on top of it? How? One way would be to take advantage of the likelihood that the consumer is in an extreme state of suggestibility that a 900-calorie liquid lunch is inadequate – that it cuts down on vital energy, perhaps sexual energy. The question then is: Can we produce a product to take advantage of the consumer's state of suggestibility? Can we produce a product that would periodically recharge his energies without adding calories? Vitamins are one answer, but they are costly and highly competitive. What we should strive for is a big mass market via an entirely new idea. Now you ask: Can we make a product that is easy to take any time of day, that can be carried in a purse or pocket, that can be bought conveniently at any store, and that can be

in which companies are diversifying into industries entirely foreign to their own, to raise the question of what America's growing diet preoccupation might mean for your company would be a legitimate question no matter what your business now is.

packaged in a way that implies unquestioned quality and medical approval?

The answer is obviously 'yes'. One possible solution is that we produce an easy-to-take, low-priced, easy-to-carry-in-pocket-or-purse dextrose tablet about the size of a cough drop. To convey the idea of quality and medical approval we would package it in a pressed-foil package of twelve tablets, each tablet individually sealed in the foil. We could promote it as a convenience item – an energy tablet for between-meal pick-ups, and without calories. And it could be advertised in ways that effectively capitalize on every one of the deep-seated psychological needs we have mentioned.

A product of this kind has actually been successfully marketed since before the Second World War in Germany by a subsidiary of Corn Products Company. Even though the promotion has been light and has emphasized the tablet's energy-giving attributes in simple straightforward terms, its success has been startling. With greater and more imaginative promotional effort, results might be spectacular.

Another significant social change, the fruits of which we are now harvesting, is what happened to American women's attitudes and values in the 1920s. Since this is a profound example of how the business executive who is sensitive to his environment can put his company in a position to act long before competition, it merits a detailed discussion.

For reasons we do not need to go into here, in the 1920s women wanted to be emancipated, to be like men. They got the franchise, bound their breasts, cut their hair, and postponed marriage. When they married they had fewer children. The birth rate dropped immensely. The depression of the 1930s prolonged this decline, in part for obvious economic reasons. Then came the Second World War with its vast manpower demands, and similarly the postwar and 1950s booms. There were huge manpower shortages, especially in the Northern cities, where both the emancipated woman and the depression had their greatest impact. The result was heavy manpower recruitment in the rural South, and a great influx of Negroes in Northern cities.

Now one unique thing about this group of Northern urban dwellers is that though it does not represent any increase in total United States population it does represent a vast increase in spending power. Not just because they get paid more in the North than the South but because for all practical purposes they really didn't get paid at all in the South. They lived off the rural land.

Looking further at this group, we see that the rate of its population increase far outstrips the national average. We see the turbulent civil-rights issues. Should you again have asked yourself whether these fundamental changes of the times had any meaning for your business? They obviously had and continue to have.

Regarding the 'emancipated' woman, she wanted first of all to be freed from the traditional symbols of her womanhood – motherhood and housewife chores. This meant she would accept faster than ever before household labour-saving devices, whether mechanical, like automatic washing machines, or more substantive, like canned foods and kindergartens. And it meant and continues to mean much more.

Regarding the growing urban Negro population, the results are so numerous and obvious it would be an insult to the reader to even discuss them.

All this shows how apparently disparate forces move implacably onward to create unexpected consequences, and that when the businessman is constantly aware of them, when he has his radar sets carefully tuned in, he may see them early and make enormous opportunities for himself.

Institutional Change. There are vast institutional changes that affect our lives and our businesses. By institutional changes we mean changes in government practices, distribution institutions like supermarkets, and service institutions like motels.

Take government, for example. The Kennedy administration was singularly dedicated to producing change. It had the energy, the imagination, the brain power, and the political savvy to carry it off. Every business should ask itself this question: How will it affect us? And not just in terms of taxes and anti-trust. It should ask: How can we capitalize on what the administration is doing and planning? It is important to ask these questions, because government action can have consequences of strange and massive proportions. Let us look at a few past examples.

In 1935 we got the Federal Old Age and Survivors Insurance programme – pensions for the retired. One result has been a real estate boom in Florida. Another result is that retired parents are no longer dependent on and live with their married children. This means that they have less influence over their grown-up children in many things these younger people do, which means that young couples are much more receptive to new ideas, new products, new ways of living. They are more free to explore and develop their own style of life because their parents no longer live with them in the same household. This affects many aspects of their lives and everybody's business. Let us continue our assumption that you are in the food-processing and packaged-foods business.

One of the things which young couples are going to experiment with more is cooking and dietary practices. It means that these young families are probably more susceptive to the idea of experimenting with new foods, new ways of preparing them, new ways of rearing children, and new eating habits. This means opportunity for you.

But while these young families are doing a lot of new dietary things, they also probably have an occasional suppressed hankering for some of the meals they fondly remember from their childhood. Food tastes we developed in our youth are extremely powerful. They linger till we die. This suggests an opportunity for foods and recipes 'like mother used to make'. In other words, opportunities are created for going into opposite directions at the same time – the new and experimental, the old and traditional. The proof of this is that, while new prepared packaged foods are selling extremely well, there is a simultaneous boom in such 'old-fashioned' foods as Pepperidge Farm bread and Duncan Hines Early American cake mixes.

The idea of a rebirth of the traditional is reinforced by other things that are happening. We have experimented so fast, we are getting so many innovations in so many things, and the traditional family is being so widely dispersed as children move to other cities far away, that many people are suddenly feeling a loss of roots, an absence of identity with traditional values. They actually crave some of the older symbols of stability, virtue, quality, and taste. This shows up in the resurging popularity of antiques, the boom of religion in the suburbs, the growing popularity of political conservatism among college students, the return of the vest in men's suits, and the new interest in the *McGuffey Reader*. So perhaps the 'like-mother-used-to-make' food idea, presented in acceptable modern dress, would be especially likely to catch on.

This new search for tradition and roots seems especially strong in young suburban families. And the reason undoubtedly is that so many of them are uprooted. They live far away from parents and relatives. They moved away, in effect, when they went off to college, after which the old hometown wasn't good enough for them any more. Since the folks back home no longer needed the supporting help of their grown children, it was legitimate for the latter to seek and get jobs in other cities. In the process they became enormously liberated from the conventions of their families. This further facilitated their freedom to develop their own food tastes, child-rearing practices, furniture choices, and other living habits.

But while they enjoy this new freedom, they also miss the old warmth and solidarity that were the comforting by-products of Sunday afternoon 'drop-in' visits by relatives and big family meals at Thanksgiving, Christmas, and other holidays. So they are now engaged in a passionate search for some sort of stability and roots. And they find them in part in 'contemporary' antiques, in barbecue togetherness, in station-wagon vacations, in apple-sauce-cake mixes, and in Little League hysteria.

To trace this all back to Old Age and Survivors Insurance is obviously ridiculous. But it certainly is an example of how government policy can help produce vast and unexpected changes. In this case, it facilitated the mobility of the American family and all that has so clearly followed.

Another government action that contributed to this mobility was the GI Bill of Rights. It made a college education widely available to millions of Americans who would otherwise have stayed at home. Once they went to college, their perambulating style of life began.

The GI bill has also irrevocably changed the hiring standards of American industry. With so many college graduates around, for a whole raft of jobs industry would suddenly talk only to college graduates. Business got so accustomed to this in just a few years, and the results were so good, that it now insists on college degrees and upgraded educations (at least high school, even for lesser jobs). The effect is that there is a great pressure on young people to go to college, and this pressure results in the demand for new government educational subsidies. The results reverberate throughout the world. For example, it provides American business with improved manpower, which makes American business more effective. This in turn forces businesses in other countries to reshape their manpower and competitive practices, universities abroad to modify their curriculums, and governments to alter their support programmes.

In part because of the boom in American education, the population is now better educated and more sophisticated than ever. And this results in part in a growth in private-label products in all lines of business. People are more self-confident about making product choices without relying so heavily on the assurance of national-brand advertising. The private-label revolution is in galloping momentum in nearly all lines of business, especially in soft goods.

It is no surprise that the private-label, so called 'discount' department store, revolution is spreading fastest in the suburbs where the better-educated people live. The fact that private-label products are priced below national brands should not deceive anyone into making the easy and erroneous generalization that their thriving success is merely a matter of price. That misses the whole point. And it overlooks the fact that the suburban dwellers are most able to pay higher prices and central urban dwellers least able. Yet it is by and large in the neighbourhoods of the former where the discount, private-label revolution is in full ascendance.

These are the ways some government actions can ripple through the economy and the world with vastly new and un-expected results. Can you predict any important future results now for what is happening in Washington and in the other capitals throughout this turbulent world?

What about the European Common Market, for example? Is it possible that it will generate such considerable movement of trade and people across old national borders that the historic national tastes and practices in food, fashion, music, laws, work habits, and distribution systems will some day become as homogenized as they are in the United States? For example, tastes are now so different between Italy and France that the Coca-Cola in Italy has to be made sweeter than in the United States, and in France dryer. Will this distinction have to be abandoned in fifteen years? If you have subsidiary companies in Europe will you have to alter your products, your distribu-tion systems, your organization, even your personal habits of dress and speech? Will the historic rationale for the ancient cartel system and all it implies be destroyed? What does this mean for your operations? What must be done now to prepare for these eventualities?

Or take Brasilia – a model city rising magnificently out of the wilderness which will put to shame any United States claim for pioneering urban progressiveness. Does it symbolize to all of South America the vast power of the State to trans-form a nation quickly – making a prophetic leap out of the nineteenth century and into the twenty-first? Will this lead to other massive efforts of a similar kind in South America and Africa – as has already been announced in Peru with the proposed opening and industrialization of the jungle plateau which is to be called, not unexpectedly, Peruvia? Doesn't all this signify tremendously important things for you? And not just obvious things either.

One thing it signifies is what we see all over the world – a rousing nationalistic awakening of long-subdued nations, a self-awareness of their own needs, their own powers, their own identities, their own destinies.

Does this in turn mean a likelihood of greater hostility to outsiders – to outside companies, and especially American corporations? This is not only a real possibility, it is a certainty.

What does it mean for you? It means everything, and not just that you have to behave less like a Yankee and more like a 'good neighbour'. It will seriously affect the kinds of products that you should be making, selling, and emphasizing in these countries if you are in them now or thinking about getting in. It means that in these newly awaking nations you should emphasize not just products from which you can make a lot of fast profits, or which merely titillate the masses (like Coca-Cola or TV sets or luxury products), but products which meet basic and obviously fundamental national needs, which help the nations achieve their desire for world position and solid economic strength. If you do that there will be less nationalistic hostility directed at you, and therefore your chances of staying in these countries and operating under less inhibiting regulatory conditions will be vastly improved.

Now let us look at the supermarket as an institution. It is a powerful agent of enormous change. Supermarkets have actually emancipated our tastes in food. They have facilitated experimentation in dietary practices, in part because of their own problems. Narrower and narrower profit margins in their traditional lines have resulted in their searching for products with wider margins. A few years ago they began stocking and prominently displaying some rather exotic delicatessen foods. People who would never have dreamed of going to a delicatessen were suddenly confronted with tempting goodies on their regular grocery shopping trips. Hesitantly they began to buy. They liked what they tasted, and now delicatessen foods are big supermarket items. Interestingly, advertising could never have created this change. For one reason, you could not advertise these items because potential volume didn't justify it. Only actual 'show' on the shelves did it.

Similarly, supermarkets have taken on classical music records and exposed them on a high-traffic basis. This in turn is doing something to the popular American taste in music.

Looking closely at the supermarket, what kinds of opportunities might it suggest for you today? It has the unique distinction of having made grocery shopping fun and interesting. Originally, there were so many interesting new items to see and explore. It was a liberating experience, especially when compared to the neighbourhood service store where you had to deal with a clerk for every single item; where you had to have a shopping list.

But all good things get tiresome. We now see that stores are getting bigger and their product lines wider. It takes more time to shop. It is harder to find things. With bigger families and more small children to take care of, the typical mother finds going to the supermarket a growing chore. A 1961 study of housewives' attitudes towards supermarket shopping revealed that they now actually think of the whole dreary process as positively irritating.

Yet what choice do they have? The Mom-and-Pop corner grocery store is an even worse place to shop. Does this mean that perhaps the supermarket has to change quite fundamentally? It most certainly does. And what does that mean for you – whether you are General Mills, or a maker of display freezers, or a producer of point-of-purchase advertising posters? We already see the growth of new food-retailing institutions – like the quick-service '7–11' stores in the South, the Bantam Supers, the superettes, and the vending-machine shopping centres such as Vendo Corporation is experimenting with in Kansas City, Esso in North Carolina, Imperial Oil in Toronto, and others are now planning in several large cities. Could it mean that we will have more compact retailing institutions, carrying fewer brands of a particular item, stocking smaller packages (or bigger packages)? How does this affect your product line?

You and Change. Change of every kind obviously affects the business firm. There are numerous ways to respond to and capitalize on change. But beyond this, business firms can themselves obviously produce change.

In each of the types of change cited above it is important to see a very powerful fact at work: you are not just a passive responder to change. You are not just a captive creature of your environment. You can perform a much more creative, satisfying, and profit-building role. *You are an active agent of your environment.* You have tremendous power to alter the competitive environment you will have to face in the future. Everything you do today becomes a fact you will have to live with tomorrow. You therefore actually *make* part of the environment in which you will operate in the future.

Of course most executives recognize that this is true when they build a new plant. It is there tomorrow to condition your competitive effectiveness. But do you recognize this when it comes to the more subtle facts of business life? Do you recognize that you can do things that alter people's habits in ways that give you enormous strength? Below are some powerful examples of how a business firm or an industry can systematically alter the general environment within which it will operate in the future.

Take the bowling business, for example. Although bowling was originally a fashionable highbrow sport, in the memory of most of us it has been considered a lowbrow, back-alley sort of recreation. Pinsetting provided intermittent employment for the lowest orders of human society – the skid-row bum. Bowling alleys were hangouts for society's drifters and wastrels.

But the automatic pinsetter changed a great deal – not simply because it eliminated the loafers and delinquents but because it was marketed with an ingenious awareness of the existing environmental barriers inside the bowling establishments themselves to the growth of bowling as a respectable mass recreation. Companies like American Machine and Foundry and Brunswick Corporation transformed the character and image of the bowling alley by developing a complete, highly upgraded package of bowling equipment and facilities that put quality, modernness, cleanliness, and even beauty into bowling. They designed everything that goes into a bowling alley (including the building layouts) so as to minimize the usual clutter and prevent the usual housekeeping bungling that detracted so much from it in the past. They purposely set out to produce a clean-cut, respectable environment within which their pinsetters were to be used.

In the end, with the felicitous help of air conditioning, bowling alleys were made so clean and attractive, and therefore bowling so respectable, that teams are now sponsored even by church groups. Parents actually encourage their subteen-age children to bowl. In order to create a better market for their bowling-alley products, what Brunswick and AMF did, in effect, was to use these products to *change the environment* in which they were to be used. The important thing to note is that it was the changed environment, *not* the greater efficiency of the automatic pinsetter, which has made automatic pin-setting and bowling the booming business they have become.

The really big-profit, big-growth-oriented company will not be satisfied merely with keeping in sufficiently flexible shape so that it can jump in the right direction when the competitive innovations of the future descend on it some fateful day. It will systematically help to create the future – resolutely dedi-cating itself to assuming the risks (and reaping the profits) of the kind of inspired leadership that has characterized the bowling-equipment companies. But to be a leader requires that we turn on our radar antenna so that we will see and hear better how the conditions of the environment in which we operate are constantly changing and producing the oppor-tunities on which leadership feeds.

Who Should Plan for Change?

An obviously critical question is this: Whose job in the organization is it to see the opportunities that are ahead? It would be easy and correct to say that it is everybody's job. And it is convenient to say that the marketing people are in an especially good position to look ahead and around because they are so close to that most important object of all business affection, the customer – the man with the money.

Certainly the marketing people are in a good position to keep their eyes peeled. But the things that are at stake for the company are too important for the highest level of management *not* to get seriously involved in. It is the unique and inescapable job of top management itself to assure the direction and destiny of the company. This means that top management must turn on its radar sets and put up its antenna more systematically than anybody else in the company. It is its job to look at the major changes in the external environment in order to see what is occurring 'out there' and what seems likely to happen five, ten, and twenty years ahead. Only top management can seriously afford to spend time thinking in such global terms. Everybody else in the company is expected to keep his nose to the current grindstone and deliver the goods today, or the company will not have a future in regard to which to make plans.

The questions that constantly need to be asked about the outside environment are as follows: How will the changes affect our company's survival power? How will they affect our opportunities? In light of what is apparently happening 'out there', what kinds of changes can we ourselves profitably initiate? But to be able to ask yourselves these questions you have to sensitize yourselves first to seeing the facts in the world, so that you can be in a position to evaluate their possible impact on you. *The first step in becoming sensitive is to recognize the importance of being sensitive.* This is perhaps the biggest step of all – the recognition on the part of top management that it has no more important duty than to become a keen observer about what lies ahead. The past is dead and gone. The present is already here but too formidable to change. But the future has neither shape nor substance. While it inescapably rises out of the present, it can to a substantial degree be moulded and manoeuvred, provided those who try have learned to see and do what is required.

We sit on a volcano of potential change. It has colossal power to alter the course of events, tastes, immemorial custom, and established ways of doing things. It has the power to immolate even the most prospering companies, companies full of outward appearances of awesome invincibility. Many companies have that invincible look, that rosy-cheeked appearance of glowing health and immortality. Yet this often turns out to be a self-deluding mask – a belief that leads to gradual decay and bankruptcy. The strongest and most prospering industry or company can die – perhaps not always with a bang, but certainly with a whimper. If it can happen to powerful nations, nations with sovereignty and military might, it can happen to companies. By comparison with nations they are like a grain of sand in the vastness of the desert.

Gradual decay and death are real possibilities for any company – not just because its management is not smart, or because it does not have able leadership or good intentions, but perhaps because individually its executives are simply not equipped to look at the external environment in the right way so that they will see the signals of change early enough. Nobody can truthfully say that the railroad executives of the early twentieth century were not able. They were indeed able managers – perhaps as a class the first really able professional managers in American industry. Yet look at the desperate condition of this once thriving 'growth' industry.

Most executives tend to think of their companies and their jobs in terms of the everyday needs and problems that demand immediate attention. A career lifetime of work in their companies has conditioned them to think in terms of their companies' internal conditions – whether it is production, finance, personnel, transportation, or even marketing. They are conditioned to think in terms of the structure and derived practices of their companies. They seldom get time to develop the skills and wide-ranging interests in the broader aspects of life to sufficiently sensitize them to the subtle developments of the external environment. Can you really see what goes on? Do you really train yourself to see and to interpret the world and its quickly changing conditions? Can you really see enough of what goes on and see it well enough to be able to respond to the hazy clues about the future which are vaguely all around us? Will you see and act on these clues early enough for your company's first-rate survival – or will the future descend upon you with shattering consequences? What are you personally doing to avoid this dismal and frightening fate – a fate that is made so imminent by the accelerating world of change in which we live?

3

MANAGEMENT MYOPIA

EVERY MAJOR industry was once a growth industry. But some that are now riding a wave of growth enthusiasm are very much in the shadow of decline. Others that are thought of as seasoned growth industries have actually stopped growing. In every case the reason growth is threatened, slowed, or stopped is not because the market is saturated. It is because there has been a failure of management.

Fateful Purposes

The failure is at the top. The executives responsible for it, in the last analysis, are those who deal with broad aims and policies. Thus:

The railroads did not stop growing because the need for passenger and freight transportation declined. That grew. The railroads are in trouble today not because the need was filled by others (cars, trucks, aeroplanes, even telephones), but because it was not filled by the railroads themselves. They let others take customers away from them because they assumed themselves to be in the railroad business rather than in the transportation business. The reason they defined their industry incorrectly was because they were railroad-oriented instead of transportation-oriented; they were product-oriented instead of customer-oriented.

Hollywood barely escaped being totally ravished by television. Actually, all the established film companies went through drastic reorganizations. Some simply disappeared. All of them got into trouble not because of TV's inroads but because of their own myopia. As with the railroads, Hollywood defined its business incorrectly. It thought it was in the movie business when it was actually in the entertainment business. 'Movies' implied a specific, limited product. This produced a fatuous contentment which from the beginning led film producers to view TV as a threat. Hollywood scorned and rejected TV when it should have welcomed it as an opportunity – an opportunity to expand the entertainment business.

Today TV is a bigger business than the old narrowly defined movie business ever was. Had Hollywood been customer-oriented (providing entertainment) rather than product-oriented (making movies), would it have gone through the fiscal purgatory that it did? I doubt it. What ultimately saved Hollywood and accounts for its recent resurgence is the wave of new young writers, producers, and directors whose previous successes in television had decimated the old movie companies and toppled the big movie moguls.

There are other less obvious examples of industries that have been and are now endangering their futures by defining their purposes improperly. I shall discuss some in detail later and analyse the kind of policies that lead to trouble. Right now it may help to show what a thoroughly customer-oriented management can do to keep a growth industry growing, even after the obvious opportunities have been exhausted; and here is one example that has been around for a long time. It is nylon – specifically, E. I. du Pont de Nemours & Company.

The company has great technical competence. Its product orientation is unquestioned. But this alone does not explain its success. After all, who was more pridefully product-oriented and product-conscious than the erstwhile New England textile companies that have been so thoroughly massacred? Du Pont has succeeded not primarily because of its product or research orientation but because it has been customer-oriented also. It is its constant watchfulness for opportunities to apply its technical know-how to the creation of customer-satisfying uses which accounts for its prodigious output of successful new products. Without a very sophisticated eye on the customer, most of its new products might have been 'wrong', its sales methods useless.

Aluminium has also continued to be a growth industry, thanks to the efforts of two wartime-created companies which deliberately set about originating new customer-satisfying uses.

Without Kaiser Aluminum & Chemical Corporation and Reynolds Metal Company, the total demand for aluminium today would be vastly smaller than it is.

Error of Analysis

Some may argue that it is foolish to set the railroads off against aluminium or the movies off against chemicals. Are not aluminium and chemicals naturally so versatile that the industries are bound to have more growth opportunities than the railroads and movies? This view commits precisely the error I have been talking about. It defines an industry, or a product, or a cluster of know-how so narrowly as to guarantee its premature senescence. When we mention 'railroads', we should make sure we mean 'transportation'. As transporters, the railroads still have a good chance for very considerable growth. They are not limited to the railroad business as such (though in my opinion rail transportation is potentially a much stronger medium than is generally believed).

What the railroads lack is not opportunity but some of the same managerial imaginativeness and audacity that made them great. Even an amateur like Jacques Barzun can see what is lacking when he says:[1]

'I grieve to see the most advanced physical and social organization of the last century go down in shabby disgrace for lack of the same comprehensive imagination that built it up. [What is lacking is] the will of the companies to survive and to satisfy the public by inventiveness and skill.'

Shadow of Obsolescence

It is impossible to mention a single major industry that did not at one time qualify for the magic appellation of 'growth industry'. In each case its assumed strength lay in the apparently unchallenged superiority of its product. There appeared to be no effective substitute for it. It was itself a runaway substitute for the product it so triumphantly replaced. Yet one after another of these celebrated industries has come

[1] Jacques Barzun, 'Trains and the Mind of Man', *Holiday*, February 1960, p. 21.

under a shadow. Let us look briefly at a few more of them, this time taking examples that have so far received a little less attention:

Dry Cleaning. This was once a growth industry with lavish prospects. In an age of wool garments, imagine finally being able to get them safely and easily cleaned. The boom was on.

Yet here we are thirty years after the boom started, and the industry is in trouble. Where has the competition come from? From a better way of cleaning? No. It has come from synthetic fibres and chemical additives that have cut the need for dry cleaning. But this is only the beginning. Lurking in the wings and ready to make chemical dry cleaning totally obsolescent is that powerful magician, ultrasonics.

Electrical Utilities. This is another one of those supposedly 'no-substitute' products which has been enthroned on a pedestal of invincible growth. When the incandescent lamp came along, kerosene lights were finished. Later the water wheel and the steam engine were cut to ribbons by the flexibility, reliability, simplicity, and just plain easy availability of electric motors. The prosperity of electrical utilities continues to wax extravagant as the home is converted into a museum of electrical gadgetry. How can anybody miss by investing in utilities, with no competition, nothing but growth ahead?

But a second look is not quite so comforting. A score of non-utility companies are well advanced towards developing a powerful chemical fuel cell which could sit in some hidden closet of every home silently ticking off electric power. The electric lines that vulgarize so many neighbourhoods will be eliminated – so will the endless demolition of streets and service interruptions during storms. Also on the horizon is solar energy, again pioneered by non-utility companies.

Who says that the utilities have no competition? They may be natural monopolies now, but tomorrow they may die natural deaths. To avoid this, they too will have to develop fuel cells, solar energy, and other power sources. To survive, they themselves will have to plot the obsolescence of what now produces their livelihood.

Grocery Stores. Many people find it hard to realize that there ever was a thriving establishment known as the 'corner grocery store'. The supermarket has taken over with a powerful effectiveness. Yet the big food chains of the 1930s narrowly escaped being completely wiped out by the aggressive expansion of independent supermarkets. The first genuine supermarket was opened in 1930, in Jamaica, Long Island. By 1933 supermarkets were thriving in California, Ohio, Pennsylvania, and elsewhere. Yet the established chains pompously ignored them. When they chose to notice them, it was with such derisive descriptions as 'cheapy', 'horse and buggy', 'cracker-barrel storekeeping', and 'unethical opportunists'.

An executive of one big chain announced at the time that he found it 'hard to believe that people will drive for miles to shop for foods and sacrifice the personal service chains have perfected and to which Mrs Consumer is accustomed'.[2] As late as 1936, the National Wholesale Grocers convention and the New Jersey Retail Grocers Association said there was nothing to fear. They said that the supers' narrow appeal to the price buyer limited the size of their market. They had to draw from miles around. When imitators came, there would be wholesale liquidations as volume fell. The current high sales of the supers was said to be partly due to their novelty. Basically people wanted convenient neighbourhood grocers. If the neighbourhood stores 'cooperate with their suppliers, pay attention to their costs, and improve their services', they would be able to weather the competition until it blew over.[3]

It never blew over. The chains discovered that survival required going into the supermarket business. This meant the wholesale destruction of their huge investments in corner-store sites and in established distribution and merchandising methods. The companies with 'the courage of their convictions' resolutely stuck to the corner-store philosophy. They kept their pride but lost their shirts.

[2] For more details see M. M. Zimmerman, *The Supermarket: A Revolution in Distribution*, McGraw-Hill Book Company, Inc, New York, 1955, p. 48.
[3] Ibid., pp. 45-7.

Self-deceiving Cycle

But memories are short. For example, it is hard for people who today confidently hail the twin messiahs of electronics and chemicals to see how things could possibly go wrong with these galloping industries. They probably also cannot see how a reasonably sensible businessman could have been as myopic as the famous Boston millionaire who fifty years ago unintentionally sentenced his heirs to poverty by stipulating that his entire estate be for ever invested exclusively in electric-streetcar securities. His posthumous declaration, 'There will always be a big demand for efficient urban transportation,' is no consolation to his heirs who sustain life by pumping gasoline at automobile filling stations.

Yet, in a casual survey I took among a group of intelligent business executives, nearly half agreed that it would be hard to hurt their heirs by tying their estates for ever to the electronics industry. When I then confronted them with the Boston streetcar example, they chorused unanimously, 'That's different!' But is it? Is not the basic situation identical?

In truth, I believe, there is no such thing as a growth industry. There are only companies organized and operated to create and capitalize on growth opportunities. Industries that assume themselves to be riding some automatic growth escalator invariably descend into stagnation. The history of every dead and dying 'growth' industry shows a self-deceiving cycle of bountiful expansion and undetected decay. There are four conditions which usually guarantee this cycle:

1. The belief that growth is assured by an expanding and more affluent population.

2. The belief that there is no competitive substitute for the industry's major product.

3. Too much faith in mass production and in the advantages of rapidly declining unit costs as output rises.

4. Preoccupation with a product that lends itself to carefully controlled scientific experimentation, improvement, and manufacturing cost reduction.

I should like now to begin examining each of these conditions in some detail. To build my case as boldly as possible, I shall illustrate the points with reference to three industries – petroleum, automotive, and electronics – particularly petroleum, because it spans more years and more vicissitudes. Not only do these three have excellent reputations with the general public and also enjoy the confidence of sophisticated investors, but their managements have become known for progressive thinking in areas like financial control, product research, and management training. If obsolescence can cripple even these industries, it can happen anywhere.

Population Myth

The belief that profits are assured by an expanding and more affluent population is dear to the heart of every industry. It takes the edge off the apprehensions everybody understandably feels about the future. If consumers are multiplying and also buying more of your product or service, you can face the future with considerably more comfort than if the market were shrinking. An expanding market keeps the manufacturer from having to think very hard or imaginatively. If thinking is an intellectual response to a problem, then the absence of a problem leads to the absence of thinking. If your product has an automatically expanding market, then you will not give much thought to how to expand it.

One of the most interesting examples of this philosophy is provided by the petroleum industry. Probably our oldest 'growth' industry, it has an enviable record. While there are some current apprehensions about its growth rate, the industry itself tends to be optimistic. But I believe it can be demonstrated that it is undergoing a fundamental yet typical change. It is not only ceasing to be a growth industry but may actually be a declining one, relative to other business. Although there is widespread unawareness of this fact, I believe that, unless it changes drastically, within twenty-five years the oil industry may find itself in much the same position of retrospective glory that the railroads are now in. Despite its pioneering work in developing and applying the present-value method of investment evaluation, in employee relations, and in working with backward countries, the petroleum business is at times a distressing example of how complacency and wrongheadedness can stubbornly convert opportunity into near disaster. Only in the last two years does it seem to have been aroused out of its heavy slumber.

One of the characteristics of this and other industries that have believed very strongly in the beneficial consequences of an expanding population, while at the same time being industries with a generic product for which there has appeared to be no competitive substitute, is that the individual companies have sought to outdo their competitors by improving on what they are already doing. This makes sense, of course, if one assumes that sales are tied to the country's population strings because the customer can compare products only on a feature-by-feature basis. Hence I believe it is very significant that not since John D. Rockefeller sent free kerosene lamps to China has the oil industry done anything really outstanding to create a demand for its product. Not even in product improvement has it showered itself with eminence. The greatest single improvement, namely, the development of tetraethyl lead, came from outside the industry, specifically from General Motors and Du Pont. The big contributions made by the industry itself are confined to the technology of oil exploration, production, and refining.

Asking for Trouble

In other words, the industry's efforts have focused not nearly so much on improving the generic product or its marketing as on improving the efficiency of getting and making its product. Moreover, its chief product has, until quite recently, continuously been defined in the narrowest possible terms, namely, gasoline, not energy, fuel, or transportation. This attitude has helped assure that:

1. Major improvements in gasoline quality in the past have tended not to originate in the oil industry itself. Also, the development of superior alternative fuels comes from outside the oil industry, as will be shown later.

2. Major innovations in automobile fuel marketing have

been originated by small new oil companies that are not primarily preoccupied with production or refining. These are the companies that have been responsible for the rapidly expanding multipump gasoline stations, with their successful emphasis on large and clean layouts, rapid and efficient driveway service, and quality gasoline at low prices.

Thus the oil industry has asked for trouble from outsiders. Sooner or later, in this land of hungry inventors and entrepreneurs, a threat is sure to come. The possibilities of this will become more apparent when we turn to the next dangerous belief of many managements. For the sake of continuity, because this second belief is tied closely to the first, I shall continue with the same example.

Idea of Indispensability

Until only two years ago the petroleum industry was pretty much persuaded that there was no competitive substitute for its major product, gasoline – or if there was, that it would continue to be a derivative of crude oil, such as diesel fuel or kerosene jet fuel.

There is a lot of automatic wishful thinking in this assumption. The trouble is that most refining companies own huge amounts of crude-oil reserves. These have value only if there is a market for products into which oil can be converted – hence the tenacious belief in the continuing competitive superiority of automobile fuels made from crude oil.

This idea persisted despite all historic evidence against it. The evidence not only shows that oil has never been a superior product for any purpose for very long but also that the oil industry has never really been a growth industry. It has been a succession of different businesses that have gone through the usual historic cycles of growth, maturity, and decay. Its overall survival is owed to a series of miraculous escapes from total obsolescence, of last-minute and unexpected reprieves from total disaster reminiscent of *The Perils of Pauline*.

Perils of Petroleum

I shall sketch in only the main episodes:

First, crude oil was largely a patent medicine. But even before that fad ran out, demand was greatly expanded by the use of oil in kerosene lamps. The prospect of lighting the world's lamps gave rise to an extravagant promise of growth. The prospects were similar to those the industry now holds for gasoline in other parts of the world. It can hardly wait for the underdeveloped nations to get a car in every garage.

In the days of the kerosene lamp, the oil companies competed with each other and against gaslight by trying to improve the illuminating characteristics of kerosene. Then suddenly the impossible happened. Edison invented a light which was totally non-dependent on crude oil. Had it not been for the growing use of kerosene in space heaters, the incandescent lamp would have completely finished oil as a growth industry at that time. Oil would have been good for little else than axle grease.

Then disaster and reprieve struck again. Two great innovations occurred, neither originating in the oil industry. The successful development of coal-burning domestic central-heating systems made the space heater obsolescent. While the industry reeled, along came its most magnificent boost yet – the internal-combustion engine, also invented by outsiders. Then when the prodigious expansion for gasoline finally began to level off in the 1920s, along came the miraculous escape of a central oil heater. Once again, the escape was provided by an outsider's invention and development. And when that market weakened, wartime demand for aviation fuel came to the rescue. After the war the expansion of civilian aviation, the dieselization of railroads, and the huge demand for cars and trucks kept the industry's growth in high gear.

Meanwhile centralized oil heating – its boom potential having only been recently proclaimed – ran into severe competition from natural gas. While the oil companies themselves owned the gas that now competed with their oil, the industry did not originate the natural-gas revolution, nor has it to this day greatly profited from its gas ownership. The gas revolution was made by newly formed transmission companies that marketed the product with an aggressive ardour. They started a magnificent new industry, first against the advice and then against the resistance of the oil companies.

By all the logic of the situation, the oil companies themselves should have made the gas revolution. They not only owned the gas; they also were the only people experienced in handling, scrubbing, and using it, the only people experienced in pipeline technology and transmission, and the only ones who understood heating problems. But partly because they knew that natural gas would compete with their own sale of heating oil, the oil companies pooh-poohed the potentials of gas.

The revolution was finally started by oil-pipeline executives who, unable to persuade their own companies to go into gas, quit and organized the spectacularly successful gas transmission companies. Even after their success became painfully evident to the oil companies, the latter did not go into gas transmission. The multibillion-dollar business which should have been theirs went to others. As in the past, the industry was blinded by its narrow preoccupation with a specific product and the value of its reserves. It paid little or no attention to its customers' basic needs and preferences.

The postwar years did not witness any change. Immediately after the Second World War the oil industry was greatly encouraged about its future by the rapid expansion of demand for its traditional line of products. In 1950 most companies projected annual rates of domestic expansion of around 6 per cent through at least 1975. Though the ratio of crude-oil reserves to demand in the free world was about 20 to 1, with 10 to 1 usually being considered a reasonable working ratio in the United States, booming demand sent oilmen searching for more without sufficient regard to what the future promised. In 1952 they 'hit' in the Middle East; the ratio skyrocketed to 42 to 1. If gross additions to reserves continue at the average rate of the past five years (37 billion barrels annually), then by 1970 the reserve ratio will be up to 45 to 1. This abundance of oil has weakened crude and product prices all over the world.

Management cannot find much consolation today in the rapidly expanding petrochemical industry, another oil-using idea that did not originate in the leading firms. The total

United States production of petrochemicals is equivalent to about 2 per cent (by volume) of the demand for all petroleum products. Although the petrochemical industry is now expected to grow by about 10 per cent per year, this will not offset other drains on the expansion of crude-oil consumption. Furthermore, while petrochemical products are many and growing, it is well to remember that there are non-petroleum sources of the basic raw material, such as coal. Besides, a lot of plastics can be produced with relatively little oil. A 50,000-barrel-per-day oil refinery is now considered the absolute minimum size for real efficiency. But a 5,000-barrel-per-day oil-using chemical plant is considered a giant operation.

Oil has never been a continuously strong growth industry. It has grown by fits and starts, always being miraculously saved by innovations and developments not of its own making. The reason it has not developed in a smooth progression is that each time it thought it had a superior product safe from the possibility of competitive substitutes, the product turned out to be inferior and notoriously subject to obsolescence. Until now, gasoline (for motor fuel, anyhow) has escaped this fate. But, as we shall see later, it too may be on its last legs.

The point of all this is that there is no guarantee against product obsolescence. If a company's own research does not make it obsolete, another's will. Unless an industry is especially lucky, as oil has been until now, it can easily go down in a sea of red figures – just as have the railroads, the buggy-whip manufacturers, the corner-grocery chains, most of the big movie companies, and indeed many others.

The best way for a firm to be lucky is to make its own luck. That requires knowing what makes a business successful. One of the greatest enemies of this knowledge is mass production.

Production Pressures

Mass-production industries are impelled by a great drive to produce all they can. The prospect of steeply declining unit costs as output rises is more than most companies can usually resist. The profit possibilities look spectacular. All effort focuses on production. The result is that marketing gets neglected.

John Kenneth Galbraith contends that just the opposite occurs.[4] Output is so prodigious that all effort concentrates on trying to get rid of it. He says this accounts for singing commercials, desecration of the countryside with advertising signs, and other wasteful and vulgar practices. Galbraith has a finger on something real, but he misses the strategic point. Mass production does indeed generate great pressure to 'move' the product. But what usually gets emphasized is selling, not marketing. Marketing, being a more sophisticated and complex process, gets ignored.

The difference between marketing and selling is more than semantic. [Selling focuses on the needs of the seller, marketing on the needs of the buyer. Selling is preoccupied with the seller's need to convert his product into cash; marketing with the idea of satisfying the needs of the customer by means of the product and the whole cluster of things associated with creating, delivering, and finally consuming it.]

In some industries the enticements of full mass production have been so powerful that for many years top management in effect has told the sales departments, 'You get rid of it; we'll worry about profits.' By contrast, a truly marketing-minded firm tries to create value-satisfying goods and services that consumers will want to buy. What it offers for sale includes not only the generic product or service but also how it is made available to the customer, in what form, when, under what conditions, and at what terms of trade. Most important, what it offers for sale is determined not by the seller but by the buyer. The seller takes his cues from the buyer in such a way that the product becomes a consequence of the marketing effort, not vice versa.

Lag in Detroit

The above may sound like an elementary rule of business, but that does not keep it from being violated wholesale. It is certainly more violated than honoured. Take the automobile industry, for example.

[4] John Kenneth Galbraith, *The Affluent Society*, Houghton Mifflin Company, Boston, 1958, pp. 152–60.

Here mass production is most famous, most honoured, and has the greatest impact on the entire society. The industry has hitched its star to the relentless requirements of the annual model change, a policy that makes customer orientation an especially urgent necessity. Consequently the auto companies spend millions of dollars a year on consumer research. But the fact that the new compact cars sold so well in the very first year of the 'Big Three's' entry into this field indicates that Detroit's vast researches had for a long time failed to reveal what the customer really wanted. Detroit was not persuaded that he wanted anything different from what he had been getting until it lost millions of customers to other small-car manufacturers.

How could this unbelievable lag behind consumer wants have been perpetuated so long? Why did not research uncover consumer preferences before consumers' buying decisions themselves revealed the facts? Is that not what consumer research is for – to find out before the fact what is going to happen? The answer is that Detroit never properly researched the customer's wants. It only investigated his preferences among the kinds of things which it had already decided to offer him. For Detroit was mainly product-oriented, not customer-oriented. To the extent that the customer was recognized as having needs that the manufacturer should try to satisfy, Detroit usually acted as if the job could be done entirely by product changes. Occasionally financing got some attention too, but that was more in order to sell than to enable the customer to buy.

As for taking care of their customer needs, there is not enough being done to write about. The areas of the greatest unsatisfied needs are ignored, or at best get stepchild attention. These areas are at the point of sale and on the matter of automotive repair and maintenance. Detroit considers these problem areas as being of secondary importance. This is underscored by the fact that the retailing and servicing ends of the industry are neither owned and operated nor controlled by the manufacturers. Once the car is produced, things are pretty much in the dealer's inadequate hands. Illustrative of Detroit's arm's-length attitude is the fact that, while servicing holds enormous sales-stimulating, profit-building opportunities, only fifty-seven of Chevrolet's 7,000 dealers provided night maintenance service in 1960.

Motorists repeatedly express their dissatisfaction with servicing and their apprehensions about buying cars under the present selling set-up. The anxieties and problems they encounter during the auto-buying and auto-maintenance processes are probably more intense and widespread today than thirty years ago. Yet the automobile companies do not seem to listen to or take their cues from the anguished consumer. If they do listen, it must be through the filter of their own preoccupation with production. The marketing effort is still viewed as a necessary consequence of the product, not vice versa, as it should be. That is the legacy of mass production, with its parochial view that profit resides essentially in low-cost full production.

What Ford Put First

The profit lure of mass production obviously has a place in the plans and strategy of business management, but it must always *follow* hard thinking about the customer. This is one of the most important lessons that we can learn from the contradictory behaviour of Henry Ford. In a sense Ford was both the most brilliant and the most senseless marketer in American history. He was senseless because he refused to give the customer anything but a black car. He was brilliant because he fashioned a production system designed to fit market needs. We habitually celebrate him for the wrong reason, his production genius. His real genius was marketing. We think he was able to cut his selling price and therefore sell millions of $500 cars because his invention of the assembly line had reduced the costs. Actually he invented the assembly line *because* he had concluded that at $500 he could sell millions of cars. Mass production was the result not the cause of his low prices.

Ford repeatedly emphasized this point, but a nation of production-oriented business managers refuses to hear the great lesson he taught. Here is his operating philosophy as he succinctly expressed it:[5]

> Our policy is to reduce the price, extend the operations, and improve the article. You will notice that the reduction of price comes first. We have never considered any costs as fixed. Therefore we first reduce the price to the point where we believe more sales will result. Then we go ahead and try to make the prices. We do not bother about the costs. The new price forces the costs down. The more usual way is to take the costs and then determine the price, and although that method may be scientific in the narrow sense, it is not scientific in the broad sense, because what earthly use is it to know the cost if it tells you that you cannot manufacture at a price at which the article can be sold? But more to the point is the fact that, although one may calculate what a cost is, and of course all of our costs are carefully calculated, no one knows what a cost ought to be. One of the ways of discovering ... is to name a price so low as to force everybody in the place to the highest point of efficiency. The low price makes everybody dig for profits. We make more discoveries concerning manufacturing and selling under this forced method than by any method of leisurely investigation.

Product Provincialism

The tantalizing profit possibilities of low unit production costs may create the most seriously self-deceiving attitude that could afflict a company, particularly a 'growth' company where an apparently assured expansion of demand already tends to undermine a proper concern for the importance of marketing and the customer.

The usual result of this narrow preoccupation with so-called 'concrete matters' is that, instead of growing, the industry declines. It usually means that the product fails to adapt to the constantly changing patterns of consumer needs and tastes, to

[5] Henry Ford, *My Life and Work*, Doubleday & Company, Inc, New York, 1923, pp. 146–7.

new and modified marketing institutions and practices, or to product developments in competing or complementary industries. The industry has its eyes so firmly on its own specific product that it does not see how it is being made obsolete.

The classical example of this is the buggy-whip industry. No amount of product improvement could stave off its death sentence. But had the industry defined itself as being in the transportation business rather than in the buggy-whip business, it might have survived. It would have done what survival always entails, that is, change. Even if it had only defined its business as providing a stimulant or catalyst to an energy source, it might have continued existence by becoming a manufacturer of, say, fanbelts or air cleaners.

What may some day be a still more classical example is, again, the oil industry. Having let others steal marvellous opportunities from it (e.g. natural gas, as already mentioned, missile fuels, and jet-engine lubricants), one would expect it to have taken steps to prevent its happening again. But this is not the case. There have been extraordinary new developments in fuel systems specifically designed to power automobiles. Not only are these developments concentrated in firms outside the petroleum industry, but until their delinquency was pointed out to them a few years ago, most petroleum companies almost systematically ignored them, securely content in their wedded bliss to oil. It is the story of the kerosene lamp versus the incandescent lamp all over again. Most big oil companies are still trying to improve hydrocarbon fuels rather than to develop fuels best suited to the needs of their users, whether or not made in different ways and with different raw materials from oil.

Here are some of the things which non-petroleum companies are working on:

Over a dozen firms now have advanced working models of energy systems which, when perfected, may very well replace the internal-combustion engine and eliminate the demand for gasoline. The superior merit of each of these systems is their elimination of frequent, time-consuming, and irritating re-fuelling stops. Most of these systems are fuel cells designed to create electric energy directly from chemicals without combustion. Most of them use chemicals that are not derived from oil, generally hydrogen and oxygen. The fact that hydrogen–oxygen systems remain crude and now entail serious combustion hazards has tranquillized most oil companies into a comforting reassurance of their own immortality.

Several non-petroleum companies have advanced models of electric storage batteries designed to power automobiles. One of these firms is an aircraft producer that is working jointly with several electrical utility companies. The latter hope to use off-peak generating capacity to supply overnight plug-in battery regeneration. Another company, also using the battery approach, is a medium-size electronics firm with extensive small-battery experience that it developed in connection with its work on hearing aids. It is collaborating with an automobile manufacturer. Recent improvements arising from the need for high-powered miniature power storage plants in rockets have put us within reach of a relatively small battery capable of withstanding great overloads or surges of power. Germanium diode applications and batteries using sintered-plate and nickel–cadmium techniques promise to make a revolution in our energy sources.

Solar energy conversion systems are also getting increasing attention. One usually cautious Detroit auto executive not long ago ventured that solar-powered cars might be common by 1980.

As for most oil companies, they are more or less 'watching developments', as one research director put it to me. Two years ago only a few were doing any research on fuel cells, and that was almost always confined to developing cells powered by hydrocarbon chemicals. None of them were enthusiastically researching fuel cells, batteries, or solar power plants. None of them were spending a fraction as much on research in these profoundly important areas as they are on the usual run-of-the-mill things like reducing combustion-chamber deposit in gasoline engines. One major integrated petroleum company not long ago took a tentative look at the fuel cell and concluded that although 'the companies actively working on it indicate a belief in ultimate success ... the timing and magnitude of its impact are too remote to warrant recognition in our forecasts'.

One might, of course, ask: Why should the oil companies do anything different? Would not chemical fuel cells, batteries, or solar energy kill the present product lines? The answer is that they would indeed, and that is precisely the reason for the oil firms having to develop these power units before their competitors, so they will not be companies without an industry.

Management might be more likely to do what is needed for its own preservation if it thought of itself as being in the energy business, as a couple of companies have now announced themselves to be. But even that is not enough if they persist in imprisoning themselves in the narrow grip of their tight product orientation. They have to think of themselves as taking care of customer needs, not finding, refining, or even selling oil. Once they genuinely think of their business as taking care of people's transportation or energy needs, nothing can stop them from creating their own extravagantly profitable growth.

'Creative Destruction'

Since words are cheap and deeds are dear, it may be appropriate to indicate what this kind of thinking involves and leads to. Let us start at the beginning – the customer. It can be shown that motorists strongly dislike the bother, delay, and experience of buying gasoline. People actually do not buy gasoline. They cannot see it, taste it, feel it, appreciate it, or really test it. What they buy is the right to continue driving their cars. The gas station is like a tax collector to whom people are compelled to pay a periodic toll as the price of using their cars. This makes the gas station a basically unpopular institution. It can never be made popular or pleasant, only less unpopular, less unpleasant.

To reduce its unpopularity completely means eliminating it. Nobody likes a tax collector, not even a pleasantly cheerful one. Nobody likes to interrupt a trip to buy a phantom product, not even from a handsome Adonis or a seductive Venus. Hence companies that are working on exotic fuel substitutes which will eliminate the need for frequent refuelling are heading directly into the outstretched arms of the irritated motorists. They are riding a wave of inevitability, not because they are creating something which is technologically superior or more sophisticated, but because they are satisfying a powerful customer need.

Once the petroleum companies recognize the customer-satisfying logic of what another power system can do, they will see that they have no more choice about working on an efficient, long-lasting fuel (or some way of delivering present fuels without bothering the motorist) than the big food chains had about going into the supermarket business, or the vacuum-tube companies had about making semiconductors. For their own good the oil firms will have to destroy their own highly profitable assets. No amount of wishful thinking can save them from the necessity of engaging in this form of 'creative destruction'.

I phrase the need as strongly as this because I think management must make quite an effort to break itself loose from conventional ways. It is all too easy in this day and age for a company or industry to let its sense of purpose become dominated by the economies of full production and to develop a dangerously lopsided product orientation. In short, if management lets itself drift, it invariably drifts in the direction of thinking of itself as producing goods and services, not customer satisfactions. While it probably will not descend to the depths of telling its salesmen, 'You get rid of it; we'll worry about profits,' it can, without knowing it, be practising precisely that formula for withering decay. The historic fate of one growth industry after another has been its suicidal product provincialism.

Dangers of R & D

Another big danger to a firm's continued growth arises when top management is wholly transfixed by the profit possibilities of technical research and development. To illustrate I shall turn first to a new industry – electronics – and then return once more to the oil companies. By comparing a fresh example with a familiar one, I hope to emphasize the prevalence and insidiousness of a hazardous way of thinking.

In the case of electronics, the greatest danger which faces the glamorous new companies in this field is not that they do not pay enough attention to research and development but that they pay too much attention to it. And the fact that the fastest-growing electronics firms owe their eminence to their heavy emphasis on technical research is completely beside the point. They have vaulted to affluence on a sudden crest of unusually strong general receptiveness to new technical ideas. Also, their success has been shaped in the virtually guaranteed market of military subsidies and by military orders that in many cases actually preceded the existence of facilities to make the products. Their expansion has, in other words, been almost totally devoid of marketing effort.

Thus they are growing up under conditions that come dangerously close to creating the illusion that a superior product will sell itself. Having created a successful company by making a superior product, it is not surprising that management continues to be oriented towards the product rather than the people who consume it. It develops the philosophy that continued growth is a matter of continued product innovation and improvement.

A number of other factors tend to strengthen and sustain this belief:

1. Because electronic products are highly complex and sophisticated, managements become top-heavy with engineers and scientists. This creates a selective bias in favour of research and production at the expense of marketing. The organization tends to view itself as making things rather than satisfying customer needs. Marketing gets treated as a residual activity, 'something else' that must be done once the vital job of product creation and production is completed.

2. To this bias in favour of product research, development, and production is added the bias in favour of dealing with controllable variables. Engineers and scientists are at home in the world of concrete things like machines, test tubes, production lines, and even balance sheets. The abstractions towards

which they feel kindly are those which are testable or manipulatable in the laboratory, or if not testable, then functional, such as Euclid's axioms. In short, the managements of the new glamour-growth companies tend to favour those business activities which lend themselves to careful study, experimentation, and control – the hard, practical, realities of the lab, the shop, the books.

What get shortchanged are the realities of the *market*. Consumers are unpredictable, varied, fickle, stupid, short-sighted, stubborn, and generally bothersome. This is not what the engineer-managers say, but deep down in their consciousness it is what they believe. And this accounts for their concentrating on what they know and what they can control, namely, product research, engineering, and production. The emphasis on production becomes particularly attractive when the product can be made at declining unit costs. There is no more inviting way of making money than by running the plant full blast.

Today the top-heavy science-engineering-production orientation of so many electronics companies works reasonably well because they are pushing into new frontiers in which the armed services have pioneered virtually assured markets. The companies are in the felicitous position of having to fill, not find, markets; of not having to discover what the customer needs and wants, but of having the customer voluntarily come forward with specific new-product demands. If a team of consultants had been assigned specifically to design a business situation calculated to prevent the emergence and development of a customer-oriented marketing viewpoint, it could not have produced anything better than the conditions just described.

Stepchild Treatment

The oil industry is a stunning example of how science, technology, and mass production can divert an entire group of companies from their main task. To the extent the consumer is studied at all, the focus is for ever on getting information which is designed to help the oil companies improve what they are now doing. Most of them generally try to discover more convincing advertising themes, more effective sales promotion drives, what the market shares of the various companies are, what people like or dislike about service-station dealers and oil companies, and so forth. Few companies seem as interested in probing deeply into the basic human needs that the industry might be trying to satisfy as in probing into the basic properties of the raw material that the companies work with in trying to deliver customer satisfactions.

Basic questions about customers and markets seldom get asked. The latter occupy a stepchild status. They are recognized as existing, as having to be taken care of, but not worth very much real thought or dedicated attention. Nobody gets as excited about the customers in his own backyard as about the oil in the Sahara Desert. Nothing illustrates better the neglect of marketing than its treatment in the industry press.

The centennial issue of the *American Petroleum Institute Quarterly*, published in 1959 to celebrate the discovery of oil in Titusville, Pennsylvania, contained twenty-one feature articles proclaiming the industry's greatness. Only one of these talked about its achievements in marketing, and that was only a pictorial record of how service-station architecture has changed. The issue also contained a special section on 'New Horizons', which was devoted to showing the magnificent role oil would play in America's future. Every reference was ebulliently optimistic, never once implying that oil might have some hard competition. Even the reference to atomic energy was a cheerful catalogue of how oil would help make atomic energy a success. There was not a single apprehension that the oil industry's affluence might be threatened or a suggestion that one 'new horizon' might include new and better ways of serving oil's present customers.

But the most revealing example of the stepchild treatment that marketing gets was still another special series of short articles on 'The Revolutionary Potential of Electronics'. Under that heading the following article titles appeared in the table of contents: 'In the Search for Oil', 'In Production Operations', 'In Refinery Processes', 'In Pipeline Operations'.

Significantly, every one of the industry's major functional areas is listed, except marketing. Why? Either it is believed that electronics holds no revolutionary potential for petroleum marketing (which is palpably wrong), or the editors forgot to discuss marketing (which is more likely and illustrates its step-child status).

The order in which the four functional areas are listed also betrays the past alienation of the oil industry from the consumer. The industry is implicitly defined as beginning with the search for oil and ending with its distribution from the refinery. But the truth is that this industry, as all industries, begins with the needs of the customer for its product. From that primal position its definition moves steadily backstream to areas of progressively lesser importance, until it finally comes to rest at the 'search for oil'.

Beginning and End

The view that an industry is a customer-satisfying process, not a goods-producing process, is vital for all businessmen to understand. An industry begins with the customer and his needs, not with a patent, a raw material, or a selling skill. Given the customer's needs, the industry develops backward, first concerning itself with the physical delivery of customer satisfactions. Then it moves back further to creating the things by which these satisfactions are in part achieved. How these materials are created is a matter of indifference to the customer; hence the particular form of manufacturing, processing, or what have you, cannot be considered as a vital aspect of the industry. Finally, the industry moves back still further to finding the raw materials necessary for making its products.

The irony of some industries oriented towards technical research and development is that the scientists who occupy the high executive positions are totally unscientific when it comes to defining their companies' overall needs and purposes. They violate the first two rules of the scientific method – being aware of and defining their companies' problems, and then developing testable hypotheses about solving them. They are scientific only about the convenient things, such as laboratory and product experiments. The reason that the customer (and the satisfaction of his deepest needs) is not considered as being 'the problem' is not because there is any certain belief that no such problem exists but because an organizational lifetime has conditioned management to look in the opposite direction. Marketing is a stepchild.

I do not mean that selling is ignored. Far from it. But selling, again, is not marketing. As already pointed out, selling concerns itself with the tricks and techniques of getting people to exchange their cash for your product. It is not concerned with the values that the exchange is all about. And it does not, as marketing invariably does, view the entire business process as consisting of a tightly integrated effort to discover, create, arouse, and satisfy customer needs. The customer is somebody 'out there' who, with proper cunning, can be separated from his loose change.

Actually, not even selling gets much attention in some technologically minded firms. Because there is a virtually guaranteed market for the abundant flow of their new products, they do not in truth know what a real market is. It is as if they lived in a planned economy, moving their products routinely from factory to retail outlet. Their successful concentration on products tends to convince them of the soundness of what they have been doing, and they fail to see the gathering clouds over the market.

Summary

Less than seventy-five years ago American railroads enjoyed a fierce loyalty among astute Wall Streeters. European monarchs invested in them heavily. Eternal wealth was thought to be the benediction for anybody who could scrape a few thousand dollars together to put into rail stocks. No other form of transportation could compete with them in speed, flexibility, durability, economy, and growth potentials. As Jacques Barzun put it, 'By the turn of the century it was an institution, an image of man, a tradition, a code of honour, a source of poetry, a nursery of boyhood desires, a sublimest of toys, and the most solemn machine – next to the funeral hearse – that marks the epochs in man's life.' [6]

[6] Op. cit., p. 20.

Even after the advent of automobiles, trucks, and aero-planes, the railroad tycoons remained imperturbably self-confident.[7] If you had told them sixty years ago that in thirty years they would be flat on their backs, broke, and pleading for government subsidies, they would have thought you totally

[7] It is true, of course, that America's railroads have been badly restricted by government regulation from going into other lines of transportation. But the record shows that those railroad companies which got into trucking, bus lines, and airlines also got out of them, and pretty much voluntarily, before the regulations got as restrictive as they did later. The railroads which went into other transport-ation media either couldn't make them pay the way railroad men wanted to see 'pay' or were unhappy about the modest regulations then in force; in some cases they actually used their operations in these media to try, in effect, to destroy their competitors therein.

The common contention that railroads were forbidden to engage in any other form of transportation is both old and incorrect. As early as 1932 the Interstate Commerce Commission laid this claim to rest when the following appeared in its *Annual Report* (pp. 21–2):

'There is no Federal prohibition of this character, except so far as the antitrust or other statutes forbid acquisitions which result in lessening of competition or restraint of trade. Nor are there any extensive State prohibitions....

'In our judgment there is great opportunity for the advan-tageous use of motor trucks and buses to supplement or in sub-stitution for railroad service, and we welcome the numerous experiments which are being made in this direction. It appears, also, that the Railway Express Agency, which is owned and con-trolled by many of the railroads collectively, has ample charter powers to use motor trucks in its operation not only in local pick-up and delivery service but also for certain line hauls, and that it is experimenting in such use. It is quite possible that this agency can be made to serve the railroads in less-than-carload freight service as well as in express package service, utilizing motor trucks to facilitate and improve such operations.

'If the railroads desire wider powers to utilize these other transportation agencies than they now possess, they should seek such powers from the appropriate legislative authorities in order that the question may receive early and thorough considera-tion.... Coordination of the various transportation agencies and their extensive use to supplement each other is highly desirable in the public interest and preferable to conditions of unrestricted competition.'

demented. Such a future was simply not considered possible. It was not even a discussable subject, or an askable question, or a matter which any sane person would consider worth speculating about. The very thought was insane. Yet a lot of 'insane' notions now have matter-of-fact acceptance – for example, the idea of 100-ton tubes of metal moving smoothly through the air 20,000 feet above the earth, loaded with a hundred sane and solid citizens casually drinking martinis. The White Queen in *Through the Looking Glass* spoke derisively about 'Some people [who] believe seven impossible things before breakfast'. But in the times we live in, this may not be such a bad thing. The failure to believe in some 'impossible' notions has dealt cruel blows to the railroads, and other industries are unknowingly waiting in line.

What specifically can companies do to avoid this fate? What does customer orientation involve? These questions have been answered in part by the preceding examples and analysis. Succeeding chapters will lay out some blueprints for action. But for now it should be obvious that building an effective customer-oriented company involves far more than good intentions or promotional tricks; it involves profound matters of human organization and leadership. For the present, let me merely suggest what appear to be some general requirements.

Visceral Feel of Greatness

Obviously the company has to do what survival demands. It has to adapt to the requirements of the market, and it has to do it sooner rather than later. But mere survival is a so-so aspiration. Anybody can survive in some way or other, even the skid-row bum. The trick is to survive gallantly, to feel the surging impulse of commercial mastery; not just to experience the sweet smell of success, but to have the visceral feel of entrepreneurial greatness.

No organization can achieve greatness without a vigorous leader who is driven onward by his own pulsating will to succeed. He has to have a vision of grandeur, a vision that can produce eager followers in vast numbers. In business the followers are the customers. To produce these customers the entire corporation must be viewed as a customer-creating and customer-satisfying organism. Management must think of itself not as producing products but as providing customer-creating value satisfactions. It must push this idea (and everything it means and requires) into every nook and cranny of the organization. It has to do this continuously and with the kind of flair that excites and stimulates the people in it. Otherwise the company will be merely a series of pigeonholed parts, with no consolidating sense of purpose or direction.

In short, the organization must learn to think of itself not as producing goods or services but as buying customers, as doing the things that will make people *want* to do business with it. And the chief executive himself has the inescapable responsibility for creating this environment, this viewpoint, this attitude, this aspiration. He himself must set the company's style, its direction, and its goals. This means he has to know precisely where he himself wants to go, and he has to make sure the whole organization is enthusiastically aware of where that is. This is a first requisite of leadership, for *unless you know where you're going, any road will take you there.*

If *any* road is all right, the chief executive might as well pack his attaché case and go fishing. If an organization does not know or care where it is going, it does not need to advertise that fact with a ceremonial figurehead. Everybody will notice it soon enough.

4

CORPORATE GOALS AND SHORT-RUN
MARKETING TACTICS

EVERY BUSINESS has two major categories of problems to which it must address policy and actions: short-run problems and long-run problems.

For the most part, the previous chapter cited examples of the ravaging consequences of various firms and industries not asking themselves some rather fundamental long-run business questions: Where is our company going? Where should it be going? What is our business, anyway?

Some companies have posthumously discovered the truth of John Maynard Keynes' statement, 'In the long run we are dead.' The tough-minded executive who shrugs off questions about the long-run direction of his company with this kind of remark says, in effect, that if we don't put all our energies into taking care of today, there won't be a tomorrow to worry about. So let's do first things first.

More will be said about this issue in the next chapter. At the moment, however, it is essential to point out that the companies which 'are dead in the long run' got that way primarily because they failed to ask themselves the questions posed above. Had they done so, they not only would have laid out the conditions and policies needed for long-run survival but would, as a consequence, have adopted day-to-day policies and practices that would have helped them more effectively to get and keep customers for their existing products and services.

The short run cannot be separated from the long run. Everything a company does today in some way locks it into some inflexible future posture, commits it to some irrevocable course of action. We know this well enough when it comes to building a plant that has a certain design, capacity, and location. But we don't always know it well enough about less tangible matters.

Thus a short-term tactic of meeting competitive prices on the head during slow times may produce tough bargaining sessions with big customers when times are brisk. Or, another example, a series of crash sales promotions or frequent new advertising campaigns will over time confuse the company's quality image such that it may gradually lose sales or have great difficulty in telling a convincing quality story when it makes a real quality breakthrough in its product.

Everything a company does today is like putting up a brick building. Every action is like a brick laid on top of other bricks that the company's policies and practices are constantly laying down. Some sort of edifice is inescapably being constructed, whether the company knows it or not. In order to avoid building a nightmare structure that will some day topple with the slightest nudge, the company, like the real-life bricklayer, needs a plan. It needs to know in detail what kind of structure it wants – what kind of structure it needs in order to survive gallantly and profitably.

Hence to know where your company is going is the first order of business. Then all policies and tactics – whether short or long range – can be fitted into the overall plan. The plan need not itself be rigid. Indeed it should not be so rigid that it cannot be modified in the periodic audits which it should undergo every few years. But at all times there must be a guiding, comprehensive scheme, or the fate of the railroads is certain to overtake it.

In order to determine where the company should be going, the following points need to be considered: (1) the company's competence – in production, marketing, management, research, finance, and material resources; (2) its history – how it got where it is, what it is known for, what it is least respected or actually criticized for; (3) its competition – who the competition is, what it is doing and not doing, how it is doing things, what it is planning; and (4) the customer – what are his needs, problems, tastes, changing wants, preferences, and expectations.

Obviously the answers to some of these questions can easily conflict with one another. Thus a company's historic competence may not be in line with the changing tastes and preferences of the customer. Or its competence may be in an area outside of the one that is required for maximum competitive effectiveness.

Thus America's basic steel manufacturers have permitted aluminium and plastics to take an incredible amount of business from them because they defined their business in terms of a historic manufacturing competence. Had they defined it in terms of their history of supplying basic fabricating materials (rather than just steel), they might have got in on the aluminium and plastics booms.

Similarly, a major American manufacturer of semiconductors was told early in 1960 that it might be a serious mistake to concentrate its research and development efforts so exclusively in solid-state physics lest developments from some other research area leave it high and dry, like the railroads. The company's PhD research director took vigorous exception to this warning, saying that, since solid-state physics encompasses about 60 per cent of nature, the company's situation was quite different from that of the railroads. It would be hard to go wrong and be caught napping by concentrating on solid-state research.

Exactly two months later many electronics companies were caught by surprise when a company outside the electronics industry announced the development of organic semiconductors that could be 'grown' like cabbages.

The point is that defining the business (the goals and the long-run direction) of a company takes more than a one-dimensional estimate of its strengths and history. Something of the kind of systematic customer-oriented thought and action that is required as a starting point is suggested in Chapters 6 and 7. At the moment let us return to the question of what genuinely customer-oriented marketing involves in the short run, that is, in connection with the products and services the company offers at present.

What Is a Product?

As pointed out earlier, the object of a company's efforts ought to be to offer a cluster of value satisfactions such that people will *want* to deal with it rather than its competitors. This involves making a careful calculation regarding what it is that the customer really values.

Thus, if you sell pianos, it is obviously critical to find out, among other things, why people buy pianos, who they buy them for, and what all the problems are in connection with using a piano. Adults buy pianos, but mostly for their children. The piano is not just a noise-making instrument or a pleasure-giving, tension-relaxing contrivance; perhaps for many buyers it is most important as a symbol of cultural elevation. They want their reluctant children to play an instrument whose presence in the house brings credit to the parents.

Furthermore, it is important to recognize the many reasons why piano sales aren't higher than they might be – such as the resistance of children, the tediousness of learning to play, the competition of hi-fi, and so forth. Hence to design a better piano, a more beautiful piano, a more compact piano, a cheaper piano, or to expand the number of retail outlets for them may be much less effective in building business than developing a faster and more congenial way of enabling people to learn to play more easily.

In today's highly competitive world, the process of getting and keeping customers requires that the generic product be *augmented* in order to sell well. That is, the product must be defined more broadly in terms of the whole cluster of satellite attributes which produce distinct customer satisfactions.

One example of how this has been done effectively is provided by Midas Mufflers. The company operates a national chain of specialty shops that sell and install automobile mufflers and tail pipes. It got to be the successful national chain it is by carefully satisfying some rather subtle customer needs.

The original theory of its president, Mr Gordon Sherman, was that people were required to undergo entirely too much inconvenience and delay in muffler and tail-pipe replacement. A job that typically took the corner service station thirty to sixty minutes could be done in ten to fifteen minutes if it were done right. Instead of laboriously unscrewing rusted clamps and holders, instead of the time-wasting pulling and tugging to separate the corroded tail pipe from the corroded muffler, instead of the motorist's being delayed by the mechanic's running out of the garage to fill another customer's gas tank, instead of the time loss involved in somebody's having to drive across town for the suitable replacement muffler – instead of all this, Sherman's idea was to apply to muffler replacement the same principle of mass production that applied to its original factory installation.

Instead of unscrewing the rusted clamps and holders, he would quickly cut them off and replace them by new ones. He would separate corroded tail pipes and mufflers the same way. And he would do everything on a quick-service, mass-production efficiency basis, at substantially reduced costs and prices. The theory was perfect, but he knew it was incomplete.

He knew that in order to operate efficiently such shops required high volume. This meant drawing customers from a much bigger radius than the conventional auto service station usually drew. Intensive advertising was clearly called for.

Here others would have stopped. Sherman did not, and therein lies the customer-oriented uniqueness of his approach. He knew his package was tremendously customer-appealing, but would they believe the ads? He reasoned that they would not, primarily because a fifteen-minute muffler change at such low prices would seem impossible, unless the mufflers were inferior and the installations shoddy. Besides, their entire experience was that a muffler replacement took thirty to sixty minutes. Perhaps it could be cut some, but not by that much.

In order to overcome this most important reaction, all new shops were designed with a catwalk running the full length of the work area with a clear glass wall facing the shop. Then the ads unambiguously told their product message, plus inviting the motorist to watch his car being worked on from a safe, clean, quiet, close-up vantage point.

The enormous success of the Midas operation speaks for itself. The important point to see is that the 'product' which Midas offered was not just low-priced mufflers, or low-priced, rapid muffler installation, but a carefully planned, fully integrated, customer-oriented package of tangible and believable value satisfactions.

Look-alike Brands

This kind of approach is becoming increasingly necessary as the distinctive features of competing generic products and brands become more fuzzy. Anybody who looks at Detroit's output today will agree that competing brands of cars are looking more and more alike. Detergents are getting more alike. So are refrigerators, washing machines, computers, machine tools, and everything else. They are getting more alike in packaging, in appearance, in versatility, in specific product features, and in the technical services which the sellers offer in connection with their products.

The customers know and the purchasing agents know that today, within any particular price line, there is precious little difference between the generic characteristics of the brands they are offered. Hence why should they buy one brand rather than another, unless its price is lower?

But for one seller to cut his price is to invite all others to do the same thing, and this leads to an infinite regress which makes only the consumer happy. It also destroys companies, after which the customer may face unhappy monopolistic conditions.

In packaged goods, the problem of product similarity leads to an incontinent variety of coupon deals, special tie-in promotions, and two-for-one sales drives. In industrial products, especially in basic commodities like steel and processed chemical raw materials, it leads to country-club romancing of purchasing agents and oversized Christmas turkeys.

The question is, what can a company do to make a prospective customer genuinely *want* to do business specifically with it so that getting rock-bottom prices is not the most important thing to which he responds? The answer obviously is to offer him things that are more important than the lowest possible price or the fact that your salesmen are particularly agile at grabbing the luncheon tab.

This gets us back to talking seriously again about the customer. Let us assume you are in an industry where the similarity of competing products is perfect, where the generic products are actually identical, such as basic chemicals. Why should a prospect want to buy from you particularly rather than from a competitor? If your quality, prices, delivery, credit arrangements, and technical services are identical, he might just as well prefer the supplier who offers the best free lunch or the biggest Christmas turkey. To get him really to *want* to deal with you so that you don't constantly have to climb down the price ladder requires that you offer him tangible benefits which he really values but which he can't get elsewhere. And to do that you have to make more of an effort to find out what he really wants and values – that is, besides what he is offered now, such as quality, price, and technical services. It means that you must seriously orient your entire operation towards discovering the customer's *total* needs and problems and then satisfying them, even if it takes you beyond what you now believe is your range of abilities and interests.

To illustrate what this kind of thoroughgoing customer orientation really involves, let us look at how it was done by one company in the fertilizer industry.

There are numerous fertilizer companies all over the country. Most of them are small and serve about a fifteen- to twenty-county area. Few companies make their own raw materials or ingredients. They buy these in bulk from big chemical manufacturers, mix them into the right proportions, and then package and sell them as ready-to-use fertilizers to co-ops, farm supply stores, and nurseries. Fertilizer plants involve only simple mixing and packaging operations.

The fertilizer companies buy their ingredients – raw potash, phosphate rock, and superphosphates – from just a handful of big bulk chemical companies. Raw-material prices charged by these suppliers tend to be identical. The range and quality of their technical services to fertilizer companies are about the same.

The marketing vice-president of one of these suppliers, International Minerals and Chemicals Corporation, a few years ago wondered how he could successfully get and keep more fertilizer companies as customers. He decided that he would have to offer prospective customers some solid reasons for dealing with his company which his competitors couldn't duplicate very quickly. But what is a solid reason? He decided to find out by commissioning a nation-wide study of the problems of fertilizer companies. The research firm he hired was told to study everything, not just production or packaging problems. After several months of interviews with these companies, the answers came. The biggest problems they seemed to have were these: figuring the sales potentials of their areas, by county; credits and collection; hiring, training, motivating, and paying salesmen; dealer training and motivation; figuring efficient shipping routes and freight costs; in-transit breakage and insurance; and advertising and sales promotion.

The upshot was that International established within its own company a management consulting organization which was made available gratis to its customers to help them in these areas. In addition it developed an easy-to-use self-help manual from which its customers could get answers to some of the above problems. Then it carefully trained its salesmen to explain and push the company's new service.

The result was that the nation's many small fertilizer companies were given a solid reason for wanting and preferring to do business with this particular supplier, whose sales promptly soared.

Products Are Value Satisfactions

Now the critical question is this: What was the product which International was now selling? To say that it was phosphates and other raw materials just isn't right. That is its generic product line. But the thing which made the company the booming success that it turned out to be was not its generic product at all. The thing which really mattered was the whole *cluster of non-product benefits* with which the company sur-rounded its generic product. Hence its success was due to a *complex bundle of value satisfactions* it offered its customers, of which the generic product was only a part – and in this case not really the most important part. Even if competitive sup-pliers had lowered their prices by a reasonably conceivable amount, they would not have substantially cut into Inter-national's sales. The reason is that International was offering an entirely *different* product from its competitors. Under-standably the competitors did not cut prices.

The operating result of International's brilliant innovation was this: Instead of it having to go out and chase customers, the customers turned around and, in effect, chased Inter-national. It was offering a cluster of value satisfactions they wanted. They *wanted* to do business with International – not because its prices were lower, not because its quality was better, not because its salesmen were nicer guys, but because it offered a 'product' its competitors were *not* offering. And International did all this not because it stumbled on it by accident but because it deliberately set out to find what the total needs and major problems of its potential customers really were. When it found out, it didn't say, 'Gee, that's too bad. Management consulting isn't our business. Besides, we don't know anything about these kinds of management prob-lems either.' Instead it said, 'Let's do what we have to do to help these people, because if we do, we will help ourselves.' And International did help itself enormously.

A similar 'cluster of value satisfactions' programme has recently been launched by the Polymer Chemicals Division of W. R. Grace & Company. Under this programme, called the 'Grace Service Plan', Grace systematically takes full-page ads in such publications as *Business Week*, offering ten major non-product-related services to its prospects and customers, including all kinds of expert merchandising and financial counselling.

An example of Grace's approach is provided by the follow-ing copy from an ad on financial counselling:

The difference between a profit and a loss often hinges on a single financial decision. Competition in plastics products is so fierce these days that how you handle your inventory control, working capital, or mold costs can change the color of the ink on your P & L statement. Your Grace representative offers financial counseling as one of the ten major services available under the Grace Service Plan. Ask him how we put that extra touch of Grace to work for you.

In 1961 a similar programme was introduced by Pillsbury Company under the banner of 'Creative Merchandising Service', or CMS.

The programme places at the disposal of the Pillsbury customer (grocers and grocery chains) what amounts to his own merchandising and advertising agency. CMS services include help in preparing newspaper, radio, or TV advertising; displays; storewide promotions; special events; or image building.

Pillsbury has a special staff to handle CMS and also makes available to customers the creative talent of Pillsbury's advertising agencies and point-of-sale suppliers.

While these services are not offered free to the customer, the customer does not actually pay with money. He merely agrees to promote a certain quantity of Pillsbury products which have been assigned value points. The 'point charge' is related to a stipulated 'point cost' of the services rendered. Six months after CMS was announced, Pillsbury was working on a constant average of two hundred requests for CMS.

Of course, one of the distinctive characteristics of the three plans described above is that each company sells to many small customers – customers who usually do not have the resources or inclination to buy or develop these services themselves.

But this hardly means that such programmes cannot effectively be offered to large companies. Large companies are usually broken down into smaller administrative and operating cells, many of which don't have but can use services which suppliers can offer. Furthermore, the supplier usually deals with only a few persons in the customer company – purchasing agents, design engineers, financial officers. These people have their special needs and problems, both personal and organizational, which suppliers should explore and try to satisfy.

Hence a purchasing agent will gain stature with his superior and, say, the engineering department when he 'finds' a supplier who offers the engineering department new and better services, or with the marketing department when he 'finds' a supplier who offers new distribution ideas and aids. Thus the purchasing agent will *want* to favour such a supplier. The other question is this: What happens if everybody offers these services? Obviously everybody will not. In any case, the object is to be first in the industry and to do it better. Moreover, to reject a new and profitable customer-getting programme because of possible imitation is simply not facing facts. The facts are that we live in a dynamic world, and if you don't do what needs to be done to get customers, somebody else will. If the fear of competitive imitation had dominated the founders and builders of your company in its beginning, chances are there wouldn't be any company today.

The International, Grace, and Pillsbury programmes are examples of customer-oriented, day-to-day marketing management at its creative best. They are distinguished by trying to have what the customer needs, not by pushing on to the customer what the seller has previously and independently decided to offer.

The development of this viewpoint regarding a company's function almost invariably requires that the seller have an open mind when defining his product since the product will always have to be something substantially more than the generic entity that issues out of the factory. When the many highly similar brands that come off the assembly lines compete for the same and increasingly more sophisticated customer, it will take more than advertising brilliance and concentrated sales push for one brand to merit the expanding favour over others. It will require offering the customer additional and distinctive value satisfactions.

The Decline of Brands

Indeed the routine emphasis on brands which has characterized competitive selling for so long is on its way out. We are now witnessing the decline of brands in the customary meaning of what brands are and do.

The most powerful indications of this are the rapid rise of so-called 'private-label' products, the booming growth of so-called 'discount department stores', and the surprising sales performances of completely unknown, little-advertised imported brands in product areas such as automobiles, typewriters, stainless-steel flatware, and transistor radios. These hard-goods sales successes are especially surprising in view of the fact that they are in product areas that have been traditionally characterized by a great deal of brand advertising and brand selling.

The discount, or self-service, department stores are equally remarkable achievements since, in their original pioneering form, they usually offered only unbranded products or unknown brands. Moreover the stores themselves were entirely new in their respective communities, with no history or 'image' to give the customer any reassurance regarding the quality or reliability of what he bought. Yet sales boomed.

The reason is largely that the modern customer is an increasingly more sophisticated and self-confident judge of product quality and reliability. He less and less requires the traditional assurances of brand advertising to help him make a choice.

That this is becoming increasingly true is reinforced by the fact that the biggest success of self-service discount department stores is being scored not in the heart of the central cities, where the lower-income groups who need to watch their pennies live, but in the suburbs. The reason is that suburban dwellers are better educated and therefore more self-confident in making product choices without the customary reassurance of a big brand label. As education expands, the traditional method of pure brand selling will become increasingly less viable.

This outlook is also reinforced by what is happening among teen-age buyers, who, while they are extremely brand conscious, are among the nation's biggest purchasers of private-label products. There is a growing and constantly more affluent teen-age population. There are more teen-agers in metropolitan Chicago than there are people living in all of San Diego or Memphis or in Newark or Indianapolis. According to a Purdue University study, three out of five teen-agers earn money from working throughout the year. One out of seven high school students earns over $15 per week. According to *Scholastic Magazine*, the average high school boy spends nearly $8 per week, and the average girl, over $5. They own impressive amounts of consumer durables: 42 per cent of the boys own electric shavers, 39 per cent of the girls own portable typewriters. Perhaps most important, over 60 per cent of the boys expect to influence their families in the next purchase of a new car.

In soft goods in particular, teen-agers are becoming the new fashion leaders, especially when it comes to sports and casual wear. They are infinitely more attracted to new casual fashions than adults, and their preferences for colour and style in these areas get reflected upward in the basic 'look' of adult styles. Where teens formerly copied the styles and colours of adults, more and more it is the other way around. It is the teens who, in effect, pioneered the big adult market in colourful casual wear. Age now follows youth, mainly because Americans of all ages increasingly want to look young, slim, and active. Even the new language of youth is becoming a status symbol when used by adults, hence the increasing adult usage of such phrases as 'how'd you make out?', 'all that jazz', and 'solid, man!'

The declining importance of brands among the opulent teen-agers plus their growing influence on adult tastes and family purchase decisions will increasingly reduce the traditional importance of branded selling. As today's teen-agers become tomorrow's parents, it will further cut into the power of the traditional brand approach to selling. It will mean greater emphasis on offering our increasingly better educated population solid value satisfactions through brands, not just routine brand reassurance.

Creating Customers for Customers

This required emphasis on solid value satisfactions extends to all types of products, not just consumer goods. That is especially so when it comes to the introduction of new industrial products. The manufacturer will not be able to rely simply on the superior virtues of his generic product. He will have to do whatever is necessary in every possible respect to make it *easy* for the prospect to buy his product. And as in the case of Henry Ford's $500 car, he will often have to 'make' a price which will fit the customer's own competitive requirements rather than simply quoting the price which his current costs seem to dictate. In order to be able to do this he will often have to *create* markets which currently do not exist.

Thus at the time when Texas Instruments sold transistors at $10 to $16 each, they had only limited applications. Hearing aids were the biggest consumer-product items. The company wanted a mass market, but its costs kept prices prohibitively high. After studying its operations, it concluded that transistors could be mass-produced to sell for as little as $2.50. The problem then was to find suitable mass-volume products for transistors. After a careful customer-oriented search, it decided that portable radios were the best bet. But since the nation's major portable producers also produced the vacuum tubes which transistors would replace, TI faced hard sledding in trying to sell the transistor portable idea to these companies.

In the end it found its only alternative was to seek out independent radio manufacturers. But since the whole proposal was so new and since most of the independents were small and unwilling or incapable of developing such small radios, TI developed the required circuit designs itself. Then it provided the other assistance that an independent manufacturer needed to bring out the first transistor radio. All told, TI invested some $2 million in this project – and built an enormously profitable mass market.

Again, this was a customer-oriented operation at its best. It demonstrates clearly why marketing must not be viewed simply as a business function but as a comprehensive view of the entire business process. As with Henry Ford, TI had a clear set of goals and took its cues from the problems of the customer, not from the economics of its existing production costs or from its historic competence. The entire corporate organism – finance, research and development, manufacturing – was altered and geared to the market's implacable requirements.

Today's Requirements versus Tomorrow's Possibilities

The chief and inescapable function of every business is getting and keeping customers. A business must learn to think of itself not as producing goods or services but as *buying customers*, as doing the things which will make people *want* to deal with it.

This does not mean that in trying to 'buy' customers a company must become a better salesman. But it will have to become a better marketer. Selling treats the customer as some anonymous creature 'out there' who, with proper handling, can be lured into your embrace and then smoothly and effectively separated from his purse. Marketing treats the customer as the original and primeval business entity – the incubator and source of your welfare and your destiny. He is what your business is all about. And that is why you must think of your business as an organized customer-creating and customer-satisfying process, as originating and delivering customer-creating value satisfactions. You need to think this way, I believe, to avoid the suicidal stagnation of merely doing *what* you've always done and of doing it *how* you've always done it. For unless you think from the beginning in the way I've been suggesting, you will create an organization that is incapable of continuously and effectively meeting the challenges that lie constantly ahead in this fast-moving, fast-changing world.

This does not mean that a company can hope to make pathbreaking progress only through fundamental long-term changes of its product line or its operating strategy. There are numerous short-range tactical possibilities available to every company to help it more effectively sell the generic products it now produces. The examples of International, Grace, and Pillsbury are clear-cut cases in point.

Every company needs to know where it wants and needs to go in the future. But it also needs to take care of the here and now. Since every action taken today affects the company's future posture, it is essential that today's action be in the context of tomorrow's plans and requirements. In either case, these requirements must be thoroughly customer-oriented. It is where the customer is that the company's present effectiveness and long-term survival lies.

Since fundamental corporate change can only be made in the long run, it is essential that the short run exhaust all possibilities for getting and keeping customers. It is all too easy for the marketing department to lay the blame for its current sales problems on product inadequacies, advertising budget limitations, and other things which require higher corporate action and long-term change. Hence a company that develops among its executives an attitude of greater introspection about its future and its goals must at the same time develop among them serious workmanlike attitudes about making the present setup work. Otherwise the possibilities for getting customers and profits today will be sacrificed to more global and interesting ruminations about the exotic possibilities of tomorrow.

5

NEEDED: MARKETING R & D

WHEN ONE business executive asks another, 'What's new?' he generally means, 'What changes are occurring that will affect business, mostly my business?' He is interested in change – specifically change that has an immediate bearing on his business. His interest usually extends to the limits imposed by his time, his capacity for easy comprehension, and the immediate relevance of change to his business today. He seldom takes much interest in the kinds of subtle changes discussed in Chapter 2. He has more immediately pressing preoccupations.

Many executives are likely to agree with the previous chapter's quotation of John Maynard Keynes, the most influential economist of this turbulent century, that 'In the long run we are dead'. They will probably echo that thought in connection with this book's call for more sensitive, long-range thinking about the subtle developments that may affect their companies' futures. They will say that all this sounds swell, but the payoff will at best be in the vague and distant future. Some executives will even suspect the whole concept of being so 'academic' that its chances of traceable payoff are, to be kind about it, at best remote. It might even turn executives into idle dreamers and away from the tangible realities of operating today's business effectively. It seems soft, flabby, unproductive, and grotesquely unbusinesslike. The operating executive understandably wants things which promise more immediate payoff.

Yet it is rare that the self-confident men who insist so strenuously on putting 'first things first' ever actually try to devise something very systematic to produce the immediate payoffs they are after, the kinds of things International

Mineral has done. When they do put first things first, these often tend to be gimmicky and transient. 'First things' tend to be crash programmes to cut costs or special promotions to raise sales. If something more lastingly substantial is done, it will usually focus on quick product innovations, on manufacturing improvements, or on organizational changes. It is rare that the critical area of marketing ever gets any of the kind of careful and continuing planning and experimental support that are so abundantly lavished on such respectable business functions as research and development or financial planning.

Yet the distinguishing characteristic of marketing is that in today's fast-moving world it uniquely comprehends the business process from the viewpoint of the influences which most clearly shape a company's future. It is the marketing view of the business process which most effectively meets the demands of a company's goals for vigorous survival because a company's survival is determined in the iron crucible of the marketplace.

A company that is weak, tardy, or sluggish in its marketing operations – and particularly if its president lacks a comprehensive marketing view of the business process – is headed for certain disaster. No wonder an official of the American Management Association recently declared, 'Every company president from 1965 on will be a marketing man' – a man who is not necessarily an experienced line marketer, but whose most outstanding attribute is that 'he thinks marketing'.

Marketing: The Neglected Stepchild

To the extent that today's marketing still does not get the continuing and systematic planning and experimental support that is lavished on other business functions, it is the neglected stepchild of most modern corporations. Most of its support is in terms of dollars and smart, fast ideas. Seldom is the support carefully systematic as in R & D. By comparison with R & D, if marketing is not a neglected stepchild, it is certainly a half-forgotten cousin.

That is a strong statement, especially in view of all today's enthusiastic talk about 'the marketing concept', the tremendous amount of expensive market research that is being done, the redundant quantities of marketing literature published, the vast number of marketing seminars being held, and the tiresome abundance of platitudinous speeches being made about marketing problems.

But none of this alters the facts. The facts are that, among the many companies whose spokesmen make such inspirational declarations about their professed marketing orientations, it is hard to find any that ever follow all this brave talk up with a solidly systematic programme of marketing experimentation and innovation. Marketing seldom gets the kind of active and continuing experimental support that other corporate functions are so abundantly getting. All it gets is money for more advertising and 'sales push'.

R & D: The False Messiah?

The big corporate experimental dollar today goes into 'research and development', which is the most lavishly endowed function in modern business. Indeed, unless a company of any size these days *has* a research and development department, it is automatically denied the right to call itself modern. R & D is treated as if it were the Messiah – the all-purpose liberator of all our painful problems.

Today R & D has a certain fad quality, though this does not alter its value. But the aims of R & D, and the benefits it produces, are essentially product- and process-oriented, not marketing-oriented. R & D does indeed often cut costs and improve and create products, and this helps a company to compete. But none of this automatically makes R & D marketing-oriented. Most people who know how R & D departments usually operate will agree that they are frequently anything but marketing-oriented. The things they do, and the people who do them, have few if any roots in what actually occurs in the market. Often they scorn the market and the customer. Often they resist the product-improvement suggestions of the marketing department and insist on working on things they personally either like or find convenient. For the marketing department to get the product planning department or the R &

D department to do the things which the market seems to be demanding often requires a lot of organizational bloodletting.

Marketing Orientation: A New Status Symbol

Within the last year or so, R & D's claim to faddish exclusiveness has begun to be challenged by narcissist corporate claims of being 'marketing-oriented'. To say this of oneself is today to achieve an automatic one-up on the competition. It produces complimentary feature articles in the trade press and is worth a couple of gratuitous points on Wall Street. Among envious competitors sitting dolefully at the sidelines, it leads to baleful self-reproach – not so much for their tardiness at not being marketing-oriented themselves, but because of their more unpardonable tardiness of not having been first in the industry to lay claim to this latest business status symbol.

Yet we often contradict in deed what we affirm in speech. We live in an age of acute managerial self-consciousness. Numerous books and articles are constantly published about what makes the manager tick. Never in the annals of modern business, going back to its Venetian origins, have businessmen been so self-consciously concerned with the way they go about their jobs. They read books and articles, enrol in executive development courses, and even solicit the candid comments of their subordinates. What emerges from this orgiastic preoccupation with self is a firm commitment to the status-giving philosophy of 'scientific management'. When nearly every executive urgently feels this pre-eminent need to be a 'scientific manager', even if only to merit the continuing good opinions of his peers and colleagues, and when the prevailing managerial orthodoxy also declares the reigning importance of being 'marketing-oriented', management will be quick indeed to get marketing-oriented – certainly at least on the verbal level.

In fact, it is on the verbal level that marketing orientation scores perhaps its only real triumph. The operational level is often indefinitely postponed. Indeed it has to be postponed because so few people seem really to understand what it entails in actual practice. The result is that the operational implementation of the marketing-oriented way of doing business seldom occurs.

Companies lyrically proclaim their marketing orientation, but for most of them it exists only on the verbal level. If it really existed on the operating level, there wouldn't be the involved inactivity and vagrant waste that characterize so many marketing departments. There wouldn't be the chaotic pulling and tugging regarding one transient and expedient policy or procedure after another. More marketing departments would have something of the same aroused frontier spirit of solid adventure and imminent breakthrough that is found in the better R & D departments. Indeed, marketing departments would do their own R & D – not in quest of new products but new marketing methods and strategies.

If the companies that are so pridefully patting themselves on their own backs about their vaunted marketing orientations were in the least bit as serious about marketing as they are about their product R & D, they would give marketing at least the equivalent qualitative kind of attention. But where are the marketing equivalents of the product R & D departments – departments specifically charged with inventing and developing marketing innovations?

The Marketing Revolution

We are, of course, now getting something close to this in a few large corporations – the marketing development department. But the job of this department is seldom viewed broadly enough. With a few notable exceptions, what this department too often does is merely assume responsibility for the company's routine market research activities, make routine long-term sales forecasts of present products, develop sales campaigns, and suggest routine product ideas based on developments in the company's laboratories or on rather commonplace analyses of competitive opportunities. What is missing is a really sensitive, continuous, imaginative analysis of business opportunities based upon systematic study of the whole society and the complex economic facts of life.

A lot of marketing changes have occurred in the last decade. Some of them are easily as dramatic and revolutionary as automation on the assembly line. Nobody in marketing needs to feel inferior in the presence of cyberneticists. There is nothing routine about such exciting marketing developments as soft-goods supermarkets, vending sales, precut meats, prepared frozen foods, motels, branch department stores, customer self-service, suburban shopping centres. Anybody who simply takes these for granted fails to recognize some of the pulsating drama of our economic times. He is blinded by the blaze of other things.

Yet with all this evidence of protean marketing activity, one sad fact stands out: few if any of these activities, or any of the other profound marketing developments that can be listed, grew out of any systematic business effort to create marketing innovations. All were either random occurrences in the bigger stream of scientific experimentation and change that characterizes our age or accidental offspring of some other facilitating development or necessity.

Current Sources of Marketing Innovation

We got concentrated frozen orange juice, for example (and its lineal descendant, the frozen-food revolution), not because somebody tried to think of a better way to help the juice customer, but because National Research Corporation, a non-food company, had developed a high-vacuum process for which it needed new markets when the declining demand for blood plasma cut its sales after the war.

While we boast that so many of today's exciting product innovations come from the laboratories of our giant corporations, it is distressing that the same companies produce so little marketing innovation. Almost every marketing innovation seems to come from tiny new companies or from companies predominantly in industries outside those in which they are innovating. These have been the facts not only in frozen orange juice and numerous precooked frozen foods but also in customer self-service of all kinds, from food supermarkets in the 1930s to soft-goods supermarkets in the 1960s; and it has been true of motels, so-called 'multipump' gasoline stations, bantam food supermarkets, and the numerous marketing changes that packaging innovations have created.

The point is that, unlike product innovations as such, most marketing innovations have been unsolicited, unplanned, accidental, and have originated from outside the central cores of the industries in which they have ultimately prospered. All this reflects a central fact of modern business: marketing is a neglected frontier.

Modern management has become aggressively innovation-minded. Most progressive companies have a vast apparatus of organized invention and innovation which is confidently expected to create the profit-building newness that was formerly the unexpected product of accidents, lonely geniuses, and intrepid master builders. Exotic new product and production methods are becoming the routine output of continuing and systematic corporate research and development. Research and development departments and product development departments are replacing advertising and public relations as the glamour functions of modern industry. Any day somebody will write a prize-winning television drama about tensions, pressures, love, and recrimination in corporate R & D, complete with menacing tycoon and ravishing blonde.

But while management is enthusiastically aware of the profit possibilities of creating entirely new and novel customer value satisfactions through new and novel products and production processes, it acts strangely unaware of the profit possibilities of creating new customer value satisfactions through entirely new and novel marketing schemes. This is especially surprising in view of repeated assertions that 'distribution is our biggest problem'.

Why No Marketing R & D?

Why do aggressive innovation-minded companies that spend so much on product research and development and abound with titles like 'New Product Development Division', 'Product Line Development Manager', 'Product Development Committee', and 'Project Team' still depend on the routine evolution of events to produce profitable new marketing ideas?

Why don't we hear more about 'marketing development departments' that are specifically charged with dreaming up and testing new marketing methods designed to fulfil specific customer needs that management or marketing research have spotted or to increase the efficiency of distribution?

Some people believe that this sort of thing is actually being done on a wide scale wherever the 'marketing concept' has been adopted. General Electric is cited as an outstanding example. But not even this pioneering company has really formalized the quest for new and improved marketing methods. Certainly it has not put forth the kind of conspicuously goal-directed innovation effort that it might.

What is badly needed, at least in our larger companies today, is the marketing equivalent of the systematic organizational attention that new product development gets. That is, something that amounts to a 'marketing development department' – a full-time, high-level group whose specific assignment is to create primarily not new products but new ways of distributing and selling existing ones. If new products result from its work (and this would be a distinct possibility), it will be because they are dictated by new marketing schemes, not vice versa, as usually happens.

But why is the marketing development department so uncommon? If a clear-cut case can be made for product research and development, it can certainly be made for the same sort of effort in marketing. Certainly no executive properly brainwashed to believe in the powerful virtues of scientific management is against marketing innovations on principle. Quite the reverse. All companies are constantly looking for new ideas. But why don't they establish some formal process to elicit them, as has been done with products and production processes?

One reason could be the fear that any such formalization might consequently formalize the environment in which marketing effort occurs. This might actually choke off the spontaneity, imaginativeness, and entrepreneurial audacity which are so important. But the chief reason probably is that the idea just has not been thought of.

The main reason for this, in turn, is that most people responsible for marketing, especially in the larger companies, do not have the kind of background or inclination which foster carefully planned experimental and speculative activity. They tend to be tough-minded day-to-day doers. Although they have become much more receptive to marketing research in recent years, there remains a strong inclination to operate on the basis of management intuition and within the limits of what has been learned by direct operating experience.

The Tyranny of Seat-of-the-Pants

While intuition and experience are powerful management skills, nobody can afford to rely on them exclusively. Yet training, conditioning, and the presumed need for fairly quick competitive manoeuvre have produced in sales management an attitude and a way of thinking that are basically inhospitable to the 'research-and-development' way of doing things. Sales management wants ideas, but it tends to want 'practical' ideas, ideas which closely conform to present ways of doing things so they can be immediately applied without inordinate strain or undue risk and which preferably produce miraculous results.

Unlike the attitude in product research and development, the quest is for speed, immediate practicality, and simplicity. No wonder the land is ravaged by such an incontinent profusion of vulgar sales gimmicks instead of more fundamental cost-reducing, customer-serving newness.

Creative Ad Agencies and Consultants

Moreover, neither the gimmicks nor such fundamental newness as does occur tends to originate in the corporation itself. They usually come from the advertising agencies and the better consulting firms. The reason the gimmicks (the slogans, posters, coupons, contests, etc.) come from the agencies is obvious. Agencies usually deal only with the product and the distribution system that have been given to them. They seldom have any power to change the basic framework within which they work. Hence they focus on the external and peripheral product symbols. But why do fundamental new ideas also originate there and among consultants?

There are two reasons. One is pure accident. The atmosphere of permissiveness that often rules at their shops (but almost never at their clients') is bound to result in some fairly good ideas, though selling them to the client is another matter. The second reason is that increasingly agencies and consultants are breaking out of their purely communications and limited project assignments and are doing 'creative' marketing research designed to uncover customer needs and, in some cases, to develop product ideas and marketing strategies, tactics, and programmes which satisfy those needs. In short, often without knowing it, some agencies and consultants are formalizing the marketing equivalent of product research and development by practising the so-called 'marketing concept'.

What the Sales Department Can't Do

Actually, it is too much to expect the sales department in the typical operating corporation to produce a lot of thoughtful innovations. It constantly has to make a good showing in its management of the present setup. The emphasis is on immediate results because that is how its performance is usually assessed. This produces an environment which develops and sustains ways of thinking that tend to legitimize the superior efficacy of the here and now. Salesmen are constantly told how wonderful they and their company are. To allow them to think otherwise, to question the superiority of the present setup, invites them to lose confidence in the organization. A salesman without confidence is not a salesman. He's a drag. He has to think and continuously be told that the present arrangement is 'the best'. Obviously this is not fertile ground for innovation.

Producer Control at Point of Sale

Another major reason why there are few if any marketing development departments, even where the idea has been discussed, is because a company cannot very easily control the ways or conditions under which its product is sold. Somebody else so often does the selling – the supermarket, the department store, the mill supply house, etc. – not the manufacturer. But in product development things are different. The soap company will try to think up and develop new products since it has full control over the ideas and their implementation. Not so in marketing. So, at least, a lot of people seem to think.

Actually the manufacturer has quite a bit of marketing control, even if he does not control the sales outlet. For example, he can do multiple-unit packaging (three bars of wrapped soap bound together), and thus he exercises some control of the method of selling. He can use display dispensers, such as sunglasses mounted on cards or paper-bound books in revolving racks. He uses transparent bubble packages to display and protect the product and cut pilferage.

Moreover, single-function franchise operations can be substantially controlled by the supplier. A case of very thorough control is the soft-ice cream drive-in establishment. Here the control of operations is achieved mainly through designing the equipment, the building, the layout, and the location in a way that optimizes the outlet's marketing effectiveness. Everything about the operation of the individual outlet has been so thoroughly planned in advance and the technology is so restrictive on the independence of the operator that even a near-illiterate can do an outstanding job of running the place effectively.

The same sort of control through planned job simplification and 'technology' is achieved in the Robert Hall clothing stores, in modern bowling establishments, and in much door-to-door selling. On the other hand, such franchise operations as gasoline stations, which could lawfully be more tightly controlled by the branded refiners, are pretty much left to be run by independent dealers in ways that often seriously detract from a brand's effectiveness and profitability.

Marketing: The Great Abstraction

A third major reason for so little systematic planning for marketing innovation is that *marketing is a fairly abstract operation*. A proposed new product's merits can be pretty easily explained and, in a way, proved even before the product reaches the drawing board. You know what you want it to do. If the various technical and material bugs can be worked out, you are reasonably sure it will perform right. A mock-up can be made to display its tangible qualities to your peers and bosses. That gives you something solid on which to pin your ideas, hopes, and salesmanship.

But in marketing, a new idea is an entirely different matter. It is stubbornly abstract. While it is easy enough to describe a new way to sell a product or service, you cannot prove it will work unless it is actually tried. The laws of physics and the principles of mechanics do not apply as they do on products. The idea cannot be tested under controlled laboratory or factory conditions. It has to be proved under the highly unstable conditions of open-market experimentation – with all the risks and uncertainties of constantly changing consumer habits, competitive retaliation, and poor or misguided management control over what is being tested. Moreover, all this testing is expensive, especially if the trial is honest and full scale, even though limited to a few test areas.

In view of these roadblocks to more imaginative marketing innovation, it seems especially important to make a formal effort to get it. That is, the harder something is to do, the more important it is to do it, and the bigger the profits if it works.

Product Gains and Marketing Lags

As a company becomes more successful in producing new and more efficient things, it becomes increasingly important for it to think more creatively and imaginatively about new marketing methods. Unless it does, its growing product profits may delude it into complacently thinking that everything is fine, when actually that is true only of part of the operation. Marketing may lag seriously. In time the profit produced by exciting new *things* may be dissipated by the inefficiency of existing old marketing *methods*.

Clearly, getting marketing innovations and marketing-oriented product innovations does not just happen by having good intentions. It also requires good men and good organization.

For the large corporation, the first step in 'good organization' is to create a setup which continuously audits the competitive and social environment within which the business will inescapably have to operate in the future so that the company can construct suitable innovation and development priorities.

The following chapter suggests an organizational approach. Chapter 7 then outlines how the people in that organizational setup should approach their job of auditing the environment. Finally Chapter 8 suggests an organizational setup for actually producing marketing innovations and marketing-oriented product innovations.

6

BLUE-SKIES PLANNING FOR BUSINESS
SURVIVAL

IN ANALYSING the future of a business, management
encounters a unique mixture of enormous uncertainties and
rare opportunities to identify and assess the cumulative
changes that inescapably affect its future. On the plus side,
management can plan to correct current policy and operating
errors; it can manoeuvre to exploit new products and market
opportunities and begin to remake the company into the kind
of organization which today it can only dream about. On the
negative side, risks mount up fast as time moves implacably
onward. The multiple vectors of social change, consumer
tastes, and product and process rationalization – these and
many more move with unexpected speed and in unpredicted
directions to make new and sometimes incredible demands on
the firm. It is one thing to speculate about these demands in
the manner of a Sunday supplement newspaper writer; it is
quite another to size them up and outline their business
implications.

The Future Is Where We Will Spend
the Rest of Our Lives

Furthermore, while thinking ahead casually as a sort of
random exercise in unrestrained speculation has certain
parlour-game attributes of idle fun, in the actual business
situation it is neither easy nor glamorous. It is serious and
risky business. Yet it is one of the most important single tasks
of every business, large or small. As Charles F. Kettering so
aptly said, 'We should all be interested in the future because
we will have to spend the rest of our lives there.' But the
future will not appear newborn on some prophetic day, like the
Messiah. It creeps up on us much as manhood creeps up on the

boy. It is constantly in an unfinished state of arrival, tantalizingly out of reach.

What is important to understand about the future is that it is always emerging from, and is part of, a panoramic amalgamation of infinitely varied forces endlessly and turbulently in motion. But since the future obviously emerges out of the present, we are in a position to predict its oncoming shape. We can do this by examining today the forces which gestate and give birth to the future. Making such predictions is a 'must' of business life. The company that does not clearly recognize, understand, and continuously chart the direction of these forces will one day find itself badly out of step and in need of drastic therapy. The American railroads are the prime and dismal example of what can happen when industry does not move with the times. And while this is a big, fat, obvious example, some of today's so-called 'progressive' companies are committing sins much like those that have landed the railroads in the desperation that is their present posture.

But predicting the future, planning a company's strategy around it, and therefore exercising some influence on the shape of the future itself, this is a difficult and risky operation. In many companies it is given little thought at all. In others it is left vicariously to engineers, research scientists, and various anonymous corporate functionaries who, hopefully, will come up with an occasional 'idea' or a hot 'hunch' around which a lot of frenetic corporate effort is quickly mobilized. In other companies it is incorrectly assumed to be the function of long-range planning groups. But these seldom do more than merely extrapolate the most obvious current market facts into some fixed point of future time. For these planners the future is almost always just a naïvely bigger version of today. Most frequently, though, future planning is casually assumed to be the chief executive's job. In practice he seldom gives more than sporadic and incomplete attention to the matter, not because he is shirking his duties but because of the press of seemingly more immediate things.

Creating a Think-ahead Attitude

How can a company systematically define and plan to meet the problems of the future? How can it do a better job of thinking ahead? I believe first of all that management must genuinely want to systematically think ahead. It has to become thoroughly convinced of its inescapable necessity. To reach that crucial state management must become more clearly aware of how rapidly and vastly the world is changing and of how little room there is for dalliance and delay.

One simple way in which the need for greater awareness of change shows up is in the rate of commercial failure of presumably obvious customer-serving new products. It is becoming more apparent daily that people don't automatically beat a path to the man with the better mousetrap. Indeed, the consumer is becoming so rapidly sophisticated that the more strident the claims of product superiority, the more likely he will suspect the opposite. The American consumer likes new and improved products and services, but he also has a lot of Yankee scepticism. He is wary of being 'made a sucker'. In his own way he is always suspending judgement and action, always doubting the hyperbolic product claim. He doesn't beat that automatic path to the purveyor of the latest new and improved mousetrap. Moreover, if science and sanitation have destroyed the mouse population, a better mousetrap is about as marketable as bonded bourbon at a Cub Scout den meeting.

Yet the country is constantly fed a flow of products and services the marketability of which is preordained to dismal failure.

Thus the Philco Corporation unveiled its slim, thin 'Predicta' line of television sets in 1958 with optimistic superlatives declaring: 'You are looking at 1960. Philco takes the most spectacular forward stride in television history. . . .' The picture tube was considerably shallower than any previous type. The line's most distinctive feature was its so-called 'screen unit' – a picture tube with a metal base – that was separate from the rest of the set. Hence the screen, which could swivel to face any direction, could be placed across the room from the cabinet containing the receiving and tuning mechanism.

Certain of these features had obvious convenience appeals for viewers. Both Philco and the trade were expansively optimistic. The initial burst of dealer enthusiasm led Philco to double production early in 1959. The fact that the Predicta's development and tooling budget had been exceeded by 25 per cent now seemed hardly worth noticing. But long before the year was over, the gloomy handwriting was on the wall: Predicta would be a colossal flop.

The basic trouble was that the general population had ceased to view the TV set exclusively as an instrument or medium of entertainment and started to view it as a piece of furniture to be properly integrated into the room. That is one reason that the furniture-styled Zenith sets were enjoying such enormous success at the time. Yet in the words of Philco's vice-president of products: 'For the first time, we had designed TV sets as instruments, distinct from furniture.' The badly burned merchandising manager of a retail chain later declared that 'people said the sets were nice to look at, but they wouldn't want to have them in their homes'.

The trouble in this, as in so many cases of new-product failures, is that somebody had not stopped to notice how things had changed in the marketplace. As we have already seen, we live in a world of rapid changes, and not only of products and processes. Public tastes, values, and wants are changing just as fast. And where they are not changing, the old ones are expressing themselves differently and operating in a changed social context. In every case of changing public tastes, values, wants, and attitudes, as will be shown later in this book, what is required is a different strategy on the part of the business firm.

It is the pre-eminent condition of business success to anticipate, evaluate, adjust to, and capitalize on the turbulent changes that so uniquely characterize our times. The firm that is not in some way aware of this necessity sentences itself to a humdrum life of passive business followership. It is always haplessly bringing up the rear, until one day it is so far behind that it quietly drops out of the parade.

We have said that it is the chief executive's unique job to look ahead and thereby help assure the continuity of the business. But in realistic practice he has many other pressing jobs. Beyond that, he seldom can hope to develop all the skills or the sensitivity to perceive adequately what the future requires in all its complex novelty. He needs people to help and guide him. In some way he must organize the company to make sure that it will see and understand the changes which are inexorably shaping society and the market in which it tries to sell. He must do this in order to avoid ruinously building a better mousetrap to catch non-existent mice. People beat a path not to the door of the man with a better mousetrap but to the door of the man who provides a cluster of value satisfactions which they prize or have been taught to esteem and want.

The purpose of this chapter is to show how a company can organize itself to anticipate change – and why this requires a different kind of approach than the normal inclinations of a company are likely to produce.

Predicting the Unknown

Regardless of the product, whether you are dealing with poorly informed housewives or with expert purchasing agents buying on specification, the process of building abiding and expanding sales is much more a matter of buying customers than of selling products. The trick is obviously to know better than your competitors what it is that will attract customers. And to do that, an essential starting point is always to ask oneself: 'What kind of society will we have in, say, five, ten, or twenty years? What does it mean for my company and its orientation?' Had the railroads asked themselves these germinal questions fifty years ago, they might now be making less frequent trips to Washington with tin cup in hand.

Usually the above questions are purposely ignored because they are so patently hard to answer. But that is exactly why it is so important to ask and answer them, and why they offer an opportunity for prodigious growth and profits for the companies that deal with them.

A company's success starts and finishes with the customer and the world he lives in. There are many things about people and society which are stable and unvarying. But for the business firm the important things are those that constantly change. While we all talk about man having a certain fixed human nature, the inescapable fact is that he is always changing. As we have seen, he changes his tastes, his preferences, his style of life, his income, where he lives, his education, and the standards by which he judges products and services. The entire society changes in the process. Unless a business constantly and carefully audits its customers, its potential customers, and their society, it will not properly anticipate the future environment in which it will have to operate. And if it does not do this critical job, it will, at best, have only a so-so future. The only way to convert this constant consciousness of the consumer and his environment into a positive and successful programme is to take periodic inventories of what is happening to the society that both shapes and is shaped by consumer tastes and fancies. Such inventories should become the basis for sound forward planning regarding the value satisfactions that the company will offer in the future and with which it will help create a prosperous future for itself.

The Blue-skies Committee

Some companies recognize the importance of anticipating and creating the future, that is, of predicting the subtle outlines of the uncertain future and then acting upon them in ways that create certain desired future conditions for themselves. One large company that manufactures and markets consumer goods tried to answer the questions of how to define and plan to meet, in this case, the marketing problems of the future, and of how to do a better job of thinking ahead. It established a special high-level committee to chart the whole spectrum of all future developments of whatever kind that might impinge on the company's marketing operations. On the basis of its findings the committee was told to develop and consider marketing 'ideas, proposals, plans, and procedures that are long-range and without regard to their immediate profitability'. The assignment letter gave the committee *carte blanche* to investigate and even recommend any marketing possibility, 'no matter how radical', that would satisfy changing consumer wants, fit the needs of expected social change, and therefore create future profit and growth opportunities for the company.

The idea for such a 'blue-skies planning committee' is a good one and deserves imitation by other companies. But there are pitfalls. In the case of the above company, the assignment was 'blue skies' in the most permissive sense of the term. Indeed, it was so permissive, and so contrary to the usual run of corporate assignments, that it turned out to be a massive failure. The reason was that most committee members failed really to understand the assignment. They did not appreciate its novelty or the magnitude of its intentions. As a consequence, they badly muffed the opportunity that was so lavishly thrust upon them.

Why Blue-skies Committees Fail

Top management blamed the committee when the assignment was improperly handled. But it was a mistake from which a lot can be learned. The fact is that failure was virtually inevitable. The assignment was simply given to the wrong people in the first place. This is a pathological condition in business – the wrong people are so often asked to do a right and necessary job. When the job doesn't get properly done, the fault is incorrectly laid to the original animating idea.

The people usually assigned to think imaginatively ahead are fairly high-level executives known for their solid accomplishments and steadfastness. When big issues and possibly new philosophies of operation are involved, it is usually felt that they should be worked out by people whose ranks equal the issues. Good as this sounds in theory, in practice it often produces waste, bad feelings, and disillusionment. If a committee so staffed produces any kind of recommendations, they are usually distinguished for their magnificent dullness. There are good reasons for this.

For one thing, men of this calibre simply do not have the training or sensitivity to chart the social or technological future. But even when they are supplied with trained social scientists as aids, their own training has made them so 'practical-minded' as to impair the effectiveness of the subordinate helpers who must work closely with them. Beyond that, these executives have a hard time thinking imaginatively ahead. They have numerous day-to-day operating responsibilities. Their regular duties require solid, responsible habits of thought and action. Even if they want to liberate themselves from such habits, chances are they do not have the time or the inclination to develop the kinds of broad-gauge personal backgrounds and interests that are necessary to do an acceptable long-range thinking job. Moreover, the jobs they are expected to do conflict with the habits of thought and action by which they have lived their entire business lives. It is asking more than is fair to require the successful line executive to transform himself at a 9.30 am meeting into a philosopher and speculator dealing with 'theoretical' propositions with seemingly remote chances of solid payoff.

His entire training has been in techniques and methods of doing *things,* not of manipulating vague ideas and complex abstractions. It is through the historic corporate system of doing things, and by the manipulation of that system, that he has reached the organizational eminence which resulted in his selection to the committee in the first place. Suddenly now he is asked to do a complete turnabout, to trade the very way of doing business that got him to where he is for something new, novel, and full of uncertainties and risks. Without knowing or intending it, he will undermine the blue-skies objectives of his assignment by continuing to think in the mould to which he attributes his success. He will depreciate the new, the novel, and the experimental, usually by constantly citing from his long and successful experience with the conventional.

Furthermore, he has himself to think about. Success for him has meant creating a reputation for sound judgement. He sees his future with the company hinging in very large part on preserving that reputation. But his new assignment calls for a completely foreign attitude. Now it is not judgement that counts, but wild audacity; not cautious consideration of businesslike alternatives, but the shotgun entertainment of radical, even harebrained notions. He is asked to adopt habits of thought and action that violate every business rule he has ever learned – habits which he knows have been the unhappy undoing of many an over-anxious young man. His dilemma is well characterized by one corporate vice-president's comments to Alex F. Osborn after being exposed to ten brainstorming sessions – where the object was for a group of ten executives gathered in a room to think of as many ways as possible to solve particular problems without regard to the immediate soundness of the solutions. Said this executive:[1]

> It was hard to get through my head what you were trying to do with us. My fifteen years of conferences in my company have conditioned me against shooting wild. Almost all of us officers rate each other on the basis of judgment – we are far more apt to look up to the other fellow if he makes no mistakes than if he suggests lots of ideas. I wish our people would feel free to shoot ideas the way we have been doing in these brainstorming sessions.

In the opinion of many observers, line officers in the military have the same weakness as operating managers in industry. They find it just as difficult, and for much the same reasons, to let their imaginations soar. For example, Dr Lloyd V. Berkner, president of Associated Universities, Inc, has pointed out that training for military command is directed primarily in terms of fighting with existing weapons, and adds:[2]

> This conditioning is a vital part of making a good fighting man; if he lets his imagination run to new and novel

[1] Alex F. Osborn, *Applied Imagination: Principles and Procedures of Creative Thinking*, Charles Scribner's Sons, New York, 1953, pp. 304–5.

[2] *Organization Administration of the Military Research and Development Programs,* Twenty-fourth Intermediate Report of the Committee on Government Operations, House Rep. No. 2618, 83d Cong., 2d Sess., 1954, p. 2.

weapons of the future, his confidence and reliance on existing weapons is shaken, and his effectiveness as a fighter is reduced. This aspect of training of good fighters has been recognized throughout history. It is, for example, stressed by Plato in his instructions for training the soldiers of The Republic. Consequently, a military officer of command calibre is quite correct in resisting thought about new weapons that subvert his fighting ability.

How to Get Blue-skies Planning

What are the implications of all this? If experienced top executives are too heavily burdened with day-to-day operating responsibilities, if their training and experiences have been too narrow, if the bases on which they have always been judged have left no room for the novel, the highly speculative, and the abstract, what can be done?

If top management wants successful blue-skies probing of the future, it must first recognize that this is something you get in ways that may be quite different from the usual ways of getting things done in the organization. Probably the best method of proceeding is to appoint a task force of carefully selected people who are known for their imaginativeness, audacity, and their rather cosmopolitan interests and competence, regardless of their positions in the official hierarchy.

One or two outside consultants might be made full-time members of the task force to give it a more panoramic flavour and a broader base. The consultants should not, however, be from the usual run of consulting firms. The trouble with most such firms is that their representatives must make their own firms look respectable. They will not 'shoot wild' either. Moreover, many consulting firms put great emphasis on quickly coming up with tangible evidence of 'progress' – and if the committee is run properly, much of its progress may not be tangible at all but consist merely of 'getting the feel for the assignment'. This would hardly do in so far as the consultants' home office is concerned.

The task force should occupy a fairly independent corporate position. It should be a separate arm of top management, with

its members having no other responsibilities. They should be
free to think and act pretty much as they please. They should
report to one top officer who recognizes that it is more important that the problem get uninhibited, full-time attention
than that immediate results be obtained. Nothing could be
worse than a set deadline. If top management has confidence
in its choice of committee members, it will let the committee
go at its own pace, although periodic consultation with the
committee can be used to indicate the desire for reasonably
early results. Actual consultation should be through the chairman and its members in fairly informal settings, such as lunch.
The idea is to create an atmosphere of open permissiveness,
with top management casually reassuring the committee that it
has confidence in its capacity to deliver the goods.

The committee's ultimate report would, primarily, be a
suggestive outline of the forces at work in the 'external'
environment (see the next chapter for details) and how these
are likely to affect the company. The actual suggestions on
how the company might be affected and how it might plan to
respond to and capitalize on these forces would be broadly
suggestive and directional, not detailed.

It is important that the committee not be expected to prepare solid or detailed proposals for long-range company
policy. Its members would probably not have the competence
for such work, nor would it be wise to make the delivery of
such proposals part of its assignment. That would merely
impede the broad-sweep thinking it is expected to do. Solid
proposals require a type of rigorous slide-rule thinking which
would circumscribe the more creative and broadly suggestive
look at the future that is the committee's primary assignment.
The actual development and analysis of specific policy proposals are a second step which should be assigned to an entirely different group. How this would be accomplished is
spelled out in Chapter 8.

When the findings are delivered, they should go directly to
top management, preferably the chief executive officer. Later
they may go down to the division and department managers

who are now so often appointed to these committees. The fact that these managers are likely to view the general blueprint of the future and its broad recommendations with misgivings, fear, or even hostile denunciation should be expected. They are not the best people to judge the appropriateness or workability of an audacious outline for the future because they are not expected to be audacious themselves.

But top management *is* expected to be. Indeed, it is one of the first duties of a man promoted to a presidency to recognize that when he reaches this stratospheric rank he must quickly unlearn many of the very things that put him there. Now he must usually be less a practical man of day-to-day affairs and more a man of vision, concerned with the big picture, dreaming dreams of what lies beyond the obvious horizon. The major part of his job is thinking far ahead. That being so, he can evaluate blue-skies proposals while his lesser but still high-level subordinates cannot. In fact, the latter hold their jobs for the express purposes of carrying out operations which the highest officials do not and often should not have time for.

Carrying Out Assignments

As emphasized before, the customer is the focus around which all business activity must ultimately centre. It is in his responses in which the company's future is reconciled. The first task of blue-skies committees, therefore, is to try to understand the customer and the society within which he does and will function in the future.

How does one go about studying and developing useful notions of what the future will look like?

One way of finding out how to do this effectively is to take a perceptive look at some of the subtle things that have happened in the recent past to shape the world we now live in, and how various industries and companies have properly or ineptly responded to these changes. This will give us some concrete examples of what I mean by 'subtle' change, 'perceptive' understanding of its meaning, and 'proper' response to it. With these illustrations in mind it will then be possible to lay out an analytical predictive scheme to guide the operations of the blue-skies committee.

The following chapter is therefore the first step towards attaining an analytical predictive scheme.

7

PLANNING AND PREPARING FOR CHANGE

EVERY STUDENT and accomplished practitioner of the art of business management agrees that it is the chief executive's unique and primary function to plan for the continuity and therefore the future of his company. But everybody also agrees that he cannot do it alone. As in all the things he does, he needs help.

This is particularly true when it comes to making essentially creative product and marketing responses to the kinds of subtle indications of distant changes that were suggested for illustrative purposes in the previous chapters.

What the chief executive needs, especially (and perhaps only) in the large corporation, is not just help. He needs a special task force or committee with the singular responsibility of perceiving, charting, and planning on capitalizing on the many social, technological, political, and competitive changes that are always in some state of imminence and arrival.

This special group is what in the previous chapter we called the 'blue-skies planning committee'. Reporting preferably to the chief executive himself, its charter is to look imaginatively into the future with the specific aim of ultimately yielding prophetic product and marketing proposals, regardless of their immediate profitability and feasibility or the historic interests and posture of the company. The idea is to create in the large organization the imaginative entrepreneurial equivalent of what is usually found in the pathbreaking small enterprise.

In order to do this unique job, the committee cannot rely on crystal balls and prophets. Its broadly suggestive proposals must rest squarely on analyses of the subtle changes in the environment within which business operates. In short, the ultimate proposals must make sense in terms of what is already happening in the world, or in terms of what reasonable men will agree is likely to happen. Indeed, unless reasonable men can in some logical fashion be convinced that it will happen, the committee will have scant chance of selling its ideas to management.

The Preliminaries

Hence the committee must examine the environment in such a way as to yield evidence out of which its proposals arise and with which it can justify them. This means that the committee must be properly staffed at the outset, or failure is certain.

But an even more certain cause of defeat is the failure of the committee to establish for itself the proper context within which to hold its deliberations. Without a clear setting it tends to go off in all kinds of ambient directions, considering a large variety of individual suggestions without regard to their relationships to each other. The committee's work generally remains on a low level of practical day-to-day operating suggestions. Seldom is solid contact made with the original assignment's call for bold, imaginative, pathbreaking proposals. The waste of time, effort, and money is stupendous. Boiled down to the bare essentials, the committee fails because:

1. It usually has not rigidly defined its objectives.

2. It usually has not stopped to identify and understand the major factors of the competitive world with which it is dealing.

The blue-skies committee must first understand that its company's business is essentially buying customers, not selling widgets. From that germinal point of view comes this principle: In order to buy customers, a company must create new value satisfactions, and this in turn emphasizes the importance of innovation in business and profit building.

Secondly, the committee must recognize that creating value satisfactions involves knowing the customer and the society. On this score its problem is much like that of the chemist in his laboratory. Before he conducts an experiment, he must know and understand the factors (or 'ingredients') he deals with, especially the following:

1. The 'external' conditions of the experiment, such as laboratory temperature, atmospheric pressure, dimensions and design of equipment, and so forth.

2. The 'internal' conditions, such as the chemicals to be mixed, their properties, how they are known to react under given circumstances, and so forth.

The commercial equivalents of these ingredients are equally important in blue-skies planning. The 'external' conditions are the society within which the company can be expected to operate in the future, that is, society's values, its technology, its arts, its tastes, its needs, its problems. The 'internal' conditions are the people of that society, their motives, their aspirations, how they react to given stimuli, how they can be taught, how they are being influenced by the 'external' conditions, and so on.

All this is very complicated, and it obviously requires people of unique capabilities. While one or two people on the committee may help the rest to see and appreciate everything that is involved and to understand its relevance to the company's product line and what that line might consist of in the future, it is important that the rest of the members have the kinds of habits of thought which will make it easier for them to accept this fairly academic and roundabout approach. Therefore both from the viewpoint of property selecting committee members and from the viewpoint of orienting them to their jobs, the vital first step is to draw up a graphically clear definition of goals and methods of approach. Otherwise the committee will not know where it is going or what is expected of it.

The committee must have a clear conception of its task and the chemist's understanding of his materials. This means a great deal of groundwork must precede any consideration of actual proposals. And this is precisely where responsible managers serving on the committee are likely to become impatient. They want solid work, not abstractions. They want proposals right away, not a lot of intellectual backing and filling. But obviously the committee has to find the basis for its work – where in broad outline it is going, and what the 'ingredients' of its materials and environment are. If it doesn't know where it is going, any proposal will do. And if it doesn't understand its materials – the customer and the society – 'any proposal' is exactly what will result.

An outline for this context – regardless of the company or industry in question – is our next topic of discussion.

A Context for the Future

For simplicity, let us confine our considerations to businesses addressing themselves to final consumers rather than to the intermediate fabricators.

Success in anticipating the future needs and responses of the consumer, and therefore success in helping to shape his needs and wants, involves two things:

1. Understanding the posture and direction of our society, how it is being shaped and modified by the forces to which it responds, and the forces it is constantly generating

2. Understanding the hidden and obvious motivations, aspirations, and needs of the consumer; the directions in which these seem to be developing; and how they both respond to and create the society which they compose.

Knowing clearly where our society is and where it is heading provides an important basis for judging the appropriateness of any plan for the future. Knowing what the consumer essentially seems to want and to what he seems to be suggestible provides an important basis for judging not only the appropriateness of a plan but also its feasibility. Most important, knowing these things, the committee is in a position to consider how to create new customers by discovering what the consumer can be taught to want.

That done, all else is easier. It provides some beginning assurances that the company, instead of being, as most are, an imitator, will become an innovator. The history of really dramatic company growth and prodigious profits is a history of innovation. The purpose of every enterprise ought to be to achieve some sort of monopoly on products or methods, however temporary it may be. That is the secret of pacesetting growth and booming profits.

What are some of the characteristics of the evolving society which we should be aware of and adjusting to?

The Social Context

Society is undergoing explosive changes in some very significant ways. The trick is to recognize what these changes are, how they are being shaped and responded to, and how they are and can be taken advantage of on the commercial front. Such things as suburbanization, casualness and informality, convenience and simplicity-oriented behaviour, the desire for efficiency and speed in all areas of activity, the extension of leisure, people's growing preoccupation with security, the upgrading of taste, perpetual prosperity – *all* these have inescapable significance for any company's future plans. Let us look at a few of these and suggest what they mean for business.

Taste. Our society's taste is being remade by the arbiters of fad and fancy. And it is not just a matter of women's fashions. It is significant that industrial designers have suddenly emerged as important functionaries in corporatedom. We don't just put a new cake mix into a corrugated box and expect people to buy it because it is good. We merchandise it, and the first step is design, of both the product and the box. And although the principles of modern graphic arts are hard for lots of people to take when it comes to abstract painting, for example, the fact is that people do like them despite a professed ignorance of or revulsion at so-called 'modern' art. Industrial designers are adopting the techniques and principles of cubist artists and putting them right on the supermarket shelf. And they sell.

Likewise architects are suddenly in huge demand. People want them to express tastes which they themselves cannot, but which they are convinced will be appreciated by those who judge them. Thus the architect's dreams become the tastes of the multitudes. Look at any modern office building or new suburb and see for yourself. Meanwhile *Life* and *Time* magazines nurture taste, regularly submitting their allegedly materialistic readers to expensively reproduced pages of modern art and long critical articles designed basically to educate the tastes of the reader.

While some industries are responding with relish to this revolution in taste, others have hardly lifted a finger. Yet the symptoms of change are all around us. What kind of house is being designed today – Victorian or California split-level? What is the rising vogue in furniture, Grand Rapids traditional or Paul McCobb Planners Group? And who is designing the reception rooms and lobbies of even the most traditional-minded corporations, the building superintendent or the graduate of the Harvard University Graduate School of Design?

But why have fancy and expensive lobbies in the first place? Obviously because top management thinks that they give the company the dignity, warmth, and modernness that people will like, so that they will want to work for or deal with the company. But if this is so, there must obviously be merit in impressing people with the same sorts of appealing stimuli in other areas where the company deals with the public. The question, therefore, that blue-skies planning must ask is this: What does contemporary taste demand; why, where does it come from; how is it developing; where is it going; and what is its significance to your company – in package design, in your letterhead design, in your calling card, in how your trucks and tank-cars are painted, in branch-office design, in product design, in your advertising?

Leisure. We hear a lot today about the vast amount of leisure time Americans have. And the demand for it grows. We are overthrowing the old puritan dictum that idleness is sin and the incubator of mischief. Not long ago the man who boasted that he had not had a vacation in ten years could confidently expect to be admired all around. Today he's likely to be thought of as either 'square' or just plain stupid. Steady, unremitting work is no longer an automatic passport to public plaudits. Leisure is legitimate.

Yet the puritan influence still remains powerful enough for us to have lingering guilt feelings about leisure. As a consequence we dress up our reference to leisure by talking not about leisure as such but about 'active leisure'. This disassociates leisure from the guilt-loaded idea of loafing. It legitimizes our abstentions from unremitting labour. Meanwhile, the work week gets shorter, and people spend more of their new leisure spending their money. A few hard-pressed or driving individuals take on second jobs and become moonlighters, but they are an unreconstructed minority.

The important thing about leisure is not that it exists, but that it alters the basic conditions of man in ways that have subtle but powerful significance to the business firm. Here are two ways in which the expansion of leisure has unexpected consequences:

1. It results in people's taking life less seriously, being more casual, and therefore more easily swayed by advertising themes that are lighthearted, gay, and have a 'fun' motif. It also means that they are more likely to respond to provocative, colourful packaging and design and to patronize retail outlets that have a more or less festive atmosphere.

2. It means that some forms of retailing which depend heavily on clerks and attendants who must work odd hours and on weekends and holidays (gasoline stations and restaurants, for example) are going to have increasing difficulty finding good workers. These people want more leisure too. And the more fetching the ads for golfing equipment, books, and weekend family barbecues, the more dissatisfied they will become with their jobs. What marketing changes does this suggest? Is the rise of the vending machine in any way related to the shortage of clerks which might result from people wanting more leisure and to work the more conventional eight-to-five hours? How does this specifically affect your business? What can you do about it – not to fight it but to capitalize on it?

Anxieties. However much people may love leisure and an easygoing life, we at the same time live in an age of anxiety. Among other things, the rapid changes which characterize our times, the dispersal of the traditional family as young people move to distant places away from their parents and the old hometown, the ideological polarization of nations, the constant radio and newspaper reminder that the world lives on the edge of constant war and revolution – these make the leisure life something less than idyllic.

The cake of custom is crumbling. It has not been replaced by any stable or predictable rules by which men can live without apprehension and uncertainty. One war and domestic crisis follows quickly after another. Minority groups are losing their old identities, and others are fighting for the traditional freedoms they have long been denied. With rapid and better-developed transportation we have become liberated from tight and direct person-to-person dependence on each other, and this has resulted in our becoming a more impersonal society. Hence we don't really 'know' our grocer the way we did in the days of the personal-service corner grocery store. We don't really know our neighbour because we really don't need him. Today we pick our friends without regard to how close they live because the car brings us close even if they live across town. At the same time, improved communication and advertising are tempting us with more wants than most of us can afford to buy, and this produces in many people a corrosive uneasiness about their frustrated wants.

All the above things, and many more, mean vast changes in society, in people's needs, and very particularly in the kinds of encompassing products and company images to which consumers will respond. This means that merchandising has new opportunities and new problems. And both promise to get bigger. One thing it means is that people take their cues regarding products less from their neighbours and parents than they used to. They make up their minds more independently.

Therefore in order to be successful, merchandising must create new kinds of psychological reassurances whenever it presents products and services to the public. Business must provide the confidence which people formerly got from close friends and family. It can do this in part through store and package design, through special product pluses, advertising, and the right kind of direct-selling devices. These in turn must provide delicacy, invitingness, deliverance from anxiety, status, aura of reliability, and relaxation. In short, the seller has to create a comforting commercial womb to which the anxious consumer will want to return.

Simplicity and Convenience. The public's desire for greater simplicity in everything it encounters is enormous, and it has great significance for every seller. Simplicity and convenience devices have already proved enormously successful in getting and keeping customers. In the automobile we see it in the automatic transmission and all kinds of power gadgets. We see it in supermarkets, both in the idea of a one-stop market and in its internal layout. In housing we find that people who do not very much care for modern design still prefer the modern over the Victorian house. For one thing, maintenance and housekeeping are much easier. Then there are suburban shopping centres, with their parking convenience; the final banishment of the potato bin in the grocery store; the popularity of drive-in movies; the trend towards push-button controls; and the triumph of zippers over buttons, the shifting patronage from hotels to motels, from walk-in central banks to drive-in branch banks, from restaurants to diners and then to drive-ins. We see it in the shift to more technically complex but operationally simpler and more convenient kitchen aids like dishwashers, automatic percolators, instant coffee, and all-purpose liquid detergents. The significant characteristic of all these developments is not labour-saving or technology or cost. It is the customer's preference for simplicity and convenience.

Certainly some simplifying changes are dictated by combinations of customer-satisfying attributes and economics, such as piggyback trucking. Some are in part dictated by manpower problems, such as dime-store supermarkets. But all reflect and help establish the pattern of simplicity and ease in our lives. What can and should the business firm do to anticipate and create more of these for its profit-building advantage? How can the way in which the product is sold – not just how it is made and packaged – capitalize on simplicity and convenience?

Speed of Service. There is a growing customer desire to be served more rapidly. The most obvious evidence of this is the growth of self-service stores and vending machines. Business establishments that operate in these ways might well advertise themselves as giving 'fast and efficient self-service'.

In a way, simplicity and speed of service are much alike; and in some cases they are combined into a single positive merchandising attribute. They capitalize on the fact that every day we are all taught at home and at work how to save time by being more efficient. The home has numerous time-saving convenience items, especially in the kitchen. The kitchen layout itself is becoming much more efficiency-oriented. At the shop and office, industrial engineers and methods engineers are all around us. The net result is that as consumers we become time-conscious.

Though we have more leisure, we seem to have less time. Our leisure-time pursuits are multiplying faster than the time available to accommodate them. Because we are becoming so thoroughly efficiency-oriented and place such a high premium on leisure activities, we are more conscious of any needless subtraction from time for these activities, of any infringement on our personally disposable time generally.

Thus in shopping, more people are substituting the telephone for the car as a shopping aid. They simply call the store and leave an order to be delivered. The American Telephone & Telegraph Company, for example, presented a report to the 1959 convention of the National Retail Merchants Association called 'What's Popping in Shopping' which showed that an aggressive programme of soliciting telephone sales in Stewart's department store in Baltimore built telephone sales, cut operating costs, and sustained the usual in-store shopping volume. As the result of this and a subsequent series of studies in other major United States department stores, it was found that for a wide range of products telephone sales actually expand total department store sales because of the greater 'convenience' to the customer. In this case 'convenience' is time-saving.

Similarly, a system of private-wire television-displayed push-button shopping is to be tried in Liberal, Kansas, by Tele-PrompTer Corporation. The viewer at home selects a demonstrated product by pushing the buttons which the announcer designates. Sizes, colours, and styles can also be indicated by the buttons. The order is automatically transmitted on to a punched card at the central station, and this moves directly to the shipping warehouse via the billing department. Next day the customer gets her item and her charge account is automatically debited.

In the repair and maintenance industries, the desire for speed may mean the substitution of huge mass-production repair centres that give fast and free pick up and delivery service for the present pattern of numerous small, conveniently located shops. Westinghouse, RAC, and Mobil Oil have already started. Thus the speed and convenience of the telephone replaces the lesser speed and convenience of many handy repair places. And in the case of Mobil Oil, at least, the rationale for establishing the first modern and technologically advanced public automotive repair and maintenance centre in history followed precisely from the kind of reasoning outlined above.

How does this public premium on speed and better use of time affect your business? What does it mean for the future of some of your present products? Does the growth of more precooked frozen and dehydrated foods, for example, predict a decline in the demand for some of your products? Will it adversely affect the market for refrigerators, sheet steel for canning, pots and pans, condiments? Will it create opportunities for, say, high-vacuum processing equipment, recreational services for housewives, gourmet restaurants for people whose culinary tastes have been upgraded by precooked gourmet foods in supermarkets?

Indeed, the restaurant business itself is in for some drastically new kinds of competition. While it would be hard to argue that the original family of TV dinners made much of an inroad on the restaurant business, the new family of precooked frozen dishes which has had such rapid public acceptance since 1960 may affect restaurants quite seriously. Food experts from all over – from the home economists in state universities to the wine-sauce connoisseurs of *Holiday* magazine – agree that these new dishes are superb by any culinary standard. If we can only now develop low-priced disposable dishes, the traditional restaurant may find itself in a declining industry.

Even now the restaurant (and also the grocery store) is facing the early possibility of competition from a remarkably thriving home-meal delivery service that was recently started in Miami Beach. The service delivers complete hot meals to people's homes on a regular route basis. The customer has a complete menu choice for each dinner meal seven days of the week. The entire ready-to-eat three-course dinner is delivered to the home at the hour specified by the customer in advance, and there is effectively guaranteed satisfaction. The price is unbelievably reasonable: $1.35 for a full filet mignon dinner, including delivery. The service was such an immediate success that in 1960 it was expanded to other cities, including New Rochelle, New York. In 1961 four more cities were added in the New York area.

Impersonality. There is a growing reduction of direct face-to-face relationships in commercial transactions. The vending machine, which doesn't talk with you, and certainly doesn't talk back, is the ultimate example – so far.

The supermarket is a less spectacular example. Now even the kindly old butcher is gone from the supermarket. It used to be argued that he would always remain because meat was one thing the housewife wanted to examine thoroughly and even to handle before buying. Meat is the core of the American diet, and therefore special care in its selection at the store was felt to enable the housewife to demonstrate her virtues as a good provider. In the face of the rise in prepared foods in supermarkets, it was felt that meat was one of the last supermarket items in connection with which she could maintain her domestic self-respect. Showing great care in its selection, perhaps even doing some haggling on cuts and trim – these were the ways she showed her friends, and more especially herself, that she was the guardian of her family's total welfare. But, alas, the butcher has gone back into the cutting room, the final victim of self-service. Given the central symbolic role of meat in the housewife's domestic round of life, how could this have happened? Understanding how it happened will help explain the central importance of the blue-skies committee's thinking along rather subtle and socially encompassing lines.

The explanation for this totally unexpected development lies deep in the changing conditions of child-rearing in America. The fact is, many young housewives are uncomfortable and uneasy in the presence of the butcher. When the reasons for this are known, it can be seen why it is so important that the blue-skies committee be composed of people who have a rather broad-ranging interest in what is going on in our society and a subtlety of perception that is understandably absent in most line executives.

Contrary to earlier generations of young women, adolescent girls today live a life of great personal freedom, mobility, and semidetachment from the family hearth. They are not so clearly dependent on their parents as formerly for education into the ways of life. They have the movies, television, highly frank and open relations with their young friends, and the freedom and mobility which the widespread teen-age ownership and use of the automobile provide. The result is the less intimate relationship of today's teen-age girls with their mothers than was true of the previous generation. Indeed, 'teen-age' is itself a new word coined for this generation. While there are now hundreds of articles listed annually under 'teen-age' in the *Readers' Guide to Periodical Literature*, twenty-five years ago the category didn't even appear.

As the result of this growing self-reliance and independence through which the new generation of young women passes during its teen years, the newly married bride does not automatically enter the role of housewife with a full store of housewifely know-how. She was never in the kitchen enough to acquire the routine skills which her mother in her own youth considered essential to womanhood. Hence she knows considerably less about kitchen affairs than our culture still seems to feel a young bride should know. The older generation's briday standards, with their emphasis on the virtues of kitchen know-how, remain resolutely with us in speech and rule-book maxims, but they are blithely ignored in practice. Today's young bride knows precious little about different kinds of meats, about various types of cuts, about their many uses, and about their required preparation time. Hence, when she goes shopping, she is much more comfortable in a self-service meat department than in a store where the presence of a butcher merely exposes her ignorance. Since rule-book maxims about what brides and all housewives should know die hard (as all such maxims do), she is embarrassed when she talks with a butcher. Hence either the butcher must be eliminated from the counter or he must be retrained to avoid embarrassing the new generation and driving it to a competing store.

What has happened at the meat counter is symptomatic of a fundamental change in commercial intercourse. Close personalization and friendliness between buyer and seller were once considered essential commercial virtues. But now they are becoming commercial vices. At most, people want simple, courteous, businesslike competence. They do not want the merchant to ask, 'How's the family?' because they know he doesn't know the family. They can quickly spot a fake, and they have learned to make decisions without a fawning salesman making all kinds of practised fuss over them. Thus one large supermarket chain which had proudly trained its employees to be 'friendly' recently discovered through depth interviews that its customers viewed them as being 'nosy'.

As pointed out previously in this book, the consumer is developing increasing self-confidence in his own judgement regarding products. He less and less needs the reassurance of a salesman or a brand. Hence he buys increasingly more non-branded and private-brand products more and more at self-service supermarkets, self-service drugstores, self-service discount centres of all kinds, and from vending machines.

These few examples of our changed and changing environment are only faint traces of the prodigious changes that lie clearly ahead. Happily, the company that is aware of them will do some audacious and imaginative forward planning to modify its products, its product line, and its whole collection of marketing techniques in ways that will reap great growth and profits. The company that sees and acts upon these changes is not simply in the position of standing ready for them when their impact arrives; it will actually help make and direct these changes. That is where the really enormous return lies.

The Customer Context

We have seen something of how the consumer or human context is being shaped and how it, in turn, shapes society. But there is a lot more to it.

In the last few years we have learned a great many mysterious and wonderful things about the shopper. We know that logic is a very minor aspect of his nature, that most of his decisions and choices are very profoundly influenced by irrational things. For example, we know that instant coffee did not sell so long as advertising merely demonstrated its ease and convenience, but that it did sell when the ads showed a contented husband drinking it. The convenience and ease were obvious, but they also gave rise to hidden guilt feelings. Housewives felt that to serve instant coffee was to confess being lazy and to not being properly devoted to the selfless care of their husbands. The idea of starting husbands off to work in the morning with a good cup of coffee has over the years become a cultural affectation. The housewife somehow feels that to fail in this is worse than gross neglect. It is nearly as bad as adultery. Hence when the ads switched from touting instant coffee's 'simplicity', 'convenience', and 'time-saving' attributes to a theme of the 'contented and admiring husband drinking instant coffee', then instant moved off the shelves fast. The new theme reassured the self-doubting housewife of the legitimacy of serving it.

Similarly, we know that advertising themes of safety, convenience, and speed addressed to businessmen did not in the early days sell air travel as well as the subsequent statement addressed to their wives which told them it would 'get him home to you sooner'. With her approval thus established, he would feel no posthumous guilt if the plane crashed; and so he flew.

We know that, although women said they wanted bigger kitchen ranges, they refused to buy them. When the same small ones were designed simply to look bigger, they sold rapidly.

We know that the low-priced car with a 'big-car door slam' ordinarily sells butter than the low-priced car with a weak-sounding slam but perhaps a better latch.

People do strange things; and they can be made to do even stranger things, provided you can find the psychological hook. They followed maniacs like Hitler as if they were sheep; for a few short weeks they nearly made General MacArthur a god; teen-age girls underwent deep emotional experiences when they watched Elvis perform. American women are repelled by painted African tribeswomen with rings in their noses but collectively spend millions of dollars each year for earrings, cosmetics, bracelets, and other 'emancipated' equivalents of nose rings; and the rest of us insist on smoking tobacco although we may fear that it stimulates cancer and are convinced that it does us no real good.

Planning and Psychology

Long-range planning must do what planning for today can do only indifferently well: it must, among other things, discover the psychological hook. It must learn what the psychological functions and overtones of products are and how these fit into the social system and the inner lives of people.

The way a product is designed and merchandised depends on many things, the most immediately important being its place on the continuum of perceived need. For example, if it is an item like cigarettes, it must obviously be marketed differently from lawn mowers. Aside from being non-essential, the cigarette choice tends to be more impulsive. It is cheaper, it has no durability, it is purchased frequently, and it competes with many other brands. Hence the package must have eye-catching distinctiveness. But whose eye: a man's, a woman's, a teen-ager's, a factory labourer's, an executive's, a white-collar worker's? If you definitely want to reach them all, what will appeal to the vast 'middle majority'? Since the choice is relatively impulsive, you want to make the product so familiar that its name is virtually burned into the smoker's mind. You want to mesmerize him with jingles and slogans, so that he will 'walk a mile for a Camel' to the cigarette counter where he will hypnotically 'call for Philip Morris' and 'sound off for Chesterfields' because 'they satisfy'. But you cannot do that with lawn mowers. The whole process is more rational and deliberate. Among other things, lawn mowers involve all kinds of prestige symbols, particularly these days when young couples are out on their suburban lawns on Saturday mornings invidiously comparing each other's garden equipment and summer foliage.

Similarly, when you sell a phantom product like gasoline (which people do not see and feel and cannot taste, compare, or adequately test), in this case, rather than trying to sell the actual product, you are compelled to sell the company and the ways and conditions under which the product is sold. This principle applies to many other products. Indeed, that is what brand-name promotion and so-called 'fair-price' legislation is all about. You are really selling the company's reputation, not its product.

The subtle ins and outs of human motivations are fascinating to observe. Take the automobile. Its purpose is obviously to provide transportation. But for many years the manufacturer who made a better car at lower prices and with lower upkeep costs could not sell his car on those claims alone. The car was, and to a large extent still is, a complex symbol. It lends and shows status; it extends people's life boundaries by giving them freedom; it gives them a feeling of pride, skill, and mastery; it bestows a sense of power for owning 'real' property; it gives real proof that the owner has adult prerogatives and capabilities; it is used to bring its owner vicarious superiority by giving more mileage, or by being the newest or the most unusual; it communicates the owner's style and taste; it celebrates important personal changes like getting married, getting a promotion, and coming of age; and it is used to express aggression through interest in horsepower, acceleration, and speed.

Cars used to have solid personalities. People would not buy a car which they felt did not express the personality they had or wanted. Thus the Cadillac remains a status car, but some people don't want it because it seems to indicate that they are pretending to be something they are not. Before the 'Forward Look', at least, Chrysler was thought of as a family car for carrying the brood around in comfort. Buick was the car of mobile and successful people interested in achieving even higher social status. That was also the image which Edsel tried so disastrously to promote. DeSoto was a conservative car, appropriate for settled people, middle-aged or retired. Dodge was viewed as sturdy, solid, and dependable, with low operating costs. And while Chevrolet was viewed as a very good solid buy, it did not have the 'animation' that was associated with the Ford. The Ford had a reputation for speed, flexibility, and durability; it had a strong appeal to young people.

In the seemingly uncomplicated days only a few years ago, before many of these strongly felt notions of a car's personality and social role eroded into painful obsolescence, if you had been an automobile manufacturer planning for the future, what personality would *you* have emphasized in the car's design and promotion? How could you have thought about making your car appeal to people with different temperaments, tastes, and needs? Was there any customer personality type not represented in the continuum of cars so that you might have tried to find and exploit it?

But more important, would you have been examining the evolving American tastes and values to try to anticipate what would appeal to the motorist in the future? Would you have permitted yourself to see that the car was losing its symbolic importance; that clothes, the home, and leisure pursuits were becoming the new status symbols for the vast middle majority of Americans? Would you have permitted your day-to-day responsibilities and the urgency of turning a profit next year – would you have allowed these to keep you from sensing that in the near future people would be looking for something entirely different from cars; not status but perhaps merely low-cost, easy, and dependable transportation, set uneasily in a continuing concern for some sort of personal distinction? Would you permit yourself even today to be perceptive enough to notice that people no longer think of themselves as car owners, but, in the words of Robert C. Hills, the business consultant, as 'car users'? And even if you noticed this change, what would it mean for you? Would you thereupon do the kinds of imaginative things which would effectively capitalize on this change of self-perception – not just in terms of advertising, but in terms of the infinitely more powerful, more profit-building, and more difficult forms of product policy, service policy, and selling methods?

The Executive's Limitations

From this sample of the context for long-run product and marketing planning it should be obvious that it is not a very good job for people who are experienced, trained, and weighed down by day-to-day operating responsibilities. They cannot easily think in these abstractions because they are doers. That is what 'executive' means: one who executes.

But executes what? Obviously there must be a plan, and the plan which produces successful and profitable innovation takes imaginative audacity. Only top management has the authority to approve plans for the distant future, and only it has the time and responsibility to deal that far ahead. But perhaps more practically, only top management can afford to be constantly and systematically visionary. Everybody below the very highest corporate rungs must keep his nose close to the operating grindstone if there is to be a corporation to execute the plan when the future arrives. All this emphasizes the need for a specialized blue-skies type of task force, certainly in the large corporation. In such a task force the right kind of broadscope thinking and directional planning can get done – done in a permissive atmosphere of disciplined speculation. And the only way to keep the group effective is for its charter to come from top management in the first place and for its reports to go to the top at all times.

Risks, Revolutions, and Rewards

A final word about the relation of the future to the present. Departing from the time-proven product and merchandising formulas of today is risky business. For this reason, of course, innovationist effort tends to be slow-moving, cautious, and not very common. Yet capitalism's unique characteristic is that it launches capital on enterprises under conditions of great economic and personal freedom. Successful capitalism requires entrepreneurship – risk taking. But most large corporations tend to be headed by managers, not entrepreneurs. Entrepreneurs create, managers execute. Where both types are present, it often produces great organizational stress. The entrepreneur wants to create, and this necessarily produces changes. The manager, on the other hand, wants to make the existing system run smoothly and efficiently – in short, to ensure the vigorous survival of the present order.

Some unfortunate cases suggest that the survival of the enterprise dictates that neither party can have his own way completely. However, the manager must ultimately yield in some way to the entrepreneur because entrepreneurship is the one essential condition of business success. Without it there is only deadening routine and finally senescence. Entrepreneurship is creativeness. It abhors sacred cows as nature abhors a vacuum. It is always creating obsolescence of something. It is engaged in 'creative destruction'. If your company is not entrepreneurial, another one will be. And because of that entrepreneurship, your company may not live long enough even to regret it. Therefore there should be no question as to whether your firm will pursue the course of the entrepreneur. It has no choice, unless it is Tiffany, whose sole stock in trade is pretty much unchanging tradition. For most of the rest, creative destruction should be the rule of life.

Being willing to destroy the old is the heart of innovation and the means to enormous profits. Alfred Sloan's inspirational introduction of the annual automobile model change demonstrates the value of creative destruction. When General Wood grafted the retail store to Sears, Roebuck and Company's thriving mail-order business, many pundits predicted an early end to the company because it was spreading itself thin. But Wood anticipated the changes which the automobile would make in rural living habits and tastes. And so while nearly everybody else barely survived the Great Depression, Sears thrived. The competitive irony of Sears' resulting triumph over Montgomery Ward is that Wood tried unsuccessfully to have Ward go in this direction while he was a young executive there. He quit and took his proposition to Sears, where its chief executive, Julius Rosenwald, welcomed it enthusiastically.

Creative destruction is a useful motto not simply because of its purposeful and ringing sound but because it creates an organizational disposition towards entrepreneurial audacity. Its constant quest is to create progress through obsolescence. Bernard Kilgore, president of the *Wall Street Journal*, has described the situation with his usual clarity:[1]

> Obsolescence is a fact, and not a theory.... Old communities will modernize or die. So will old industries.
> The real challenge in all this is the opportunity of one of the new frontiers of the future that does not look like a frontier at all. It is the opportunity to tear down and rebuild in a new pattern a very large segment of America that we today are likely to regard as 'already built'.

The attitude of creative destruction can only be incubated and preserved if a company's highest officials create for their company a permissive atmosphere for audacious experimentation. And they must be willing to make mistakes. Lawrence Appley of the American Management Association has summarized the point neatly:[2]

> An entire organization will reflect top management's basic attitude towards the making of mistakes. If top management is intent upon making real progress, it has certainly learned that progress entails a certain amount of error. That attitude is essential to a dynamic, hard-hitting, high-moraled, and successful organization.

[1] Bernard Kilgore, 'Business Tomorrow: A Long Range Look at Its Prospects and Problems', *Changing Patterns in Distribution*, American Management Association, New York, 1952, p. 21.

[2] Lawrence A. Appley, *Management in Action*, American Management Association, New York, 1956, p. 41.

But in accepting and fostering the attitude of creative destruction, top management must also recognize the setting in which the attitude is to govern. There must be a closely reasoned context. No matter what may be involved in the organizational interval between the chief executive and the ultimate consumer, in the end the most relevant context is that of society and the customer. Unless these are studied and understood, and unless everything that is done is fitted into the scheme that they imply, planning for the future will be essentially sterile. The planners will operate in a luminous fog, depending on outmoded maxims, generalizing from particularistic experiences, and usually ending up with some sort of ceremonial affirmation of the present. Inertia will have won a dismal and ravaging victory.

That is why a blue-skies task force to scan the context systematically can be so useful. From the above examples of the usefulness of looking at the social and consumer contexts it is clear that the task force's job is a special kind of job for special people. And through periodic 'context audits' of the kind that has been suggested, it can provide the basis for the right kind of detailed planning for future growth and profits. It will do this because it will be providing the kind of basic information about the likely configuration of the future without which planning for the future is little more than seat-of-the-pants guesswork. In the perceptive words of Marion Harper, Jr, 'To manage a business well is to manage its future; and to manage the future is to manage information.'[3]

[3] Marion Harper, Jr, 'A New Profession to Aid Marketing Management', *Journal of Marketing*, January 1961, p. 1.

8

THE MARKETING DEVELOPMENT DEPARTMENT

REGARDLESS OF the number of decentralized centres of entrepreneurial initiative in the large corporation, the palpable fact of its massive size has an inescapable conservatizing influence. It tends to produce conventionality in people, in ideas, in operating practices. Nowhere is this more true than in marketing, where pathbreaking innovational achievements among large corporations are notably non-existent.

With the blue-skies task force doing its work competently, the large corporation at last will get some of the powerful profit-building insights into the future which have always been the distinctive output of men of business genius.

With these insights now available to it on a regular basis, the large corporation at last has a thoroughly marketing-oriented basis for developing the long-range customer-getting marketing and product innovations which booming business survival requires in this fast-moving age. The marketing development department proposed in Chapter 5 is now in a position to suggest and produce the pathbreaking innovations that make for business greatness.

The question is: Where do you start? How do you set up a marketing development department? What instructions should it get? What kind of people should serve on it? How does it fit into the corporate setup? To whom should it report? How does it operate?

Who Should Handle Marketing Development?

Any management which wants this kind of an operation must first recognize that this is uncompromisingly an area of top management responsibility. The operation will not work unless it has powerful top management sponsorship and continuing support.

Second, the job of formalizing marketing progress cannot be entrusted to some existing operating group – say, the sales promotion department. Indeed, the most important and most troublesome problem that will arise will be selecting the members of the marketing development department itself.

This is the pre-eminent problem. It is virtually impossible to be too careful in selecting them. One mistake, and the whole effort may be ruined. Everything hinges on the type of man entrusted to run the department – much more so than in a product development department. Basically, the department must be headed and staffed by operating people who are at home in the world of abstractions and ideas.

The successful administration of a marketing development department involves different kinds of attitudes and viewpoints than does a product R & D department. In recent years most of us have become accustomed to expecting as a matter of routine rapid changes and improvements in industry's physical output. Indeed we view this as a necessity. Most responsible people in the typical modern corporation strongly favour and look for product and process innovation. Hence the product development department operates in a highly permissive corporate environment. It is expected to produce change – any kind of change. In this new age of scientific wonders it is a rare and reckless man who says that a new product proposal, no matter how wild-eyed it may seem, is indeed wild-eyed. As was noted in Chapter 5, science and technology are treated as the new Messiah – the all-purpose wonder-worker that will solve all our problems, the Mr Clean of the corporate household.

By contrast, we are likely to be more suspicious (or, at best, less trusting) of a new marketing proposal. It is an abstraction the utility of which is debatable and not provable except after the fact. Besides, it may threaten the security of those who are in charge of and operate the present marketing setup. They will therefore resist improvement ideas that might obsolesce the operating procedures, organizational routine, and sales philosophy which they manipulate and to which they owe their present corporate eminence. Hence the company environment that the marketing development people work in will seldom be very permissive. Without strong personal convictions and drive, and without strong top management support, they can easily fail.

One thing is clear: the marketing development department must be staffed by energetic people who have no corporate or strong personal ties to, or interests in, perpetuating the present marketing scheme. They must not be put into the position of jeopardizing their own personal futures because they are pushing ideas which may offend or threaten people who are in a position to affect their careers. In short, the greatest care must be taken to free them from inhibiting attitudes to change.

Besides being at home in the world of ideas, they must also be the kind of people who can effectively use the information and suggestions produced by the blue-skies planning group. They must have an active and solidly demonstrated interest in the broadest spectrum of the business view of life; the physical, social, and life sciences; aesthetics; mass culture; and technology. In short, they must have a restless need to be on top of things – of the whole panoramic cluster of ideas, theories, facts, and events that constantly reshape our lives, tastes, values, and needs. They must be the type of people who regularly read widely and avidly and exhibit an enthusiastic flair for business. Granted that this is a big order, consider the following examples:

A national chain of franchised service stores has hired humanities professors away from colleges and made them, in effect, territorial sales managers. The operation has been prodigiously successful, in the fastest possible time. The company president attributes much of the company's success to the unique talents which these unusual managers have brought to the training, supervision, and counselling of its store.

A large industrial chemicals company was looking around for new chemical-using product ideas to suggest to various capital and consumer goods industries. It solicited ideas from within its ranks by circulating an open letter which was also published in the company's several house organs. The volume of responses was overwhelming. Of course there were a lot of 'half-baked' ideas. But some revealed an extraordinary range of talents in their originators. Some were so well thought out and were accompanied with such complete background material and such masterly analyses of the difficult production and subtle marketing methods that the products required that their authors – some of them completely unheard of organizationally – were quickly marked as 'comers' and given more challenging jobs.

To Whom to Report

The marketing development department must not be made responsible to persons, or to committees composed of persons, who are immediately and directly involved in the day-to-day administration of the present marketing setup. It should report directly to a high corporate officer – preferably the marketing vice-president or an executive vice-president – somebody whose regular corporate duties are of a policy nature rather than concerned with day-to-day operations.

The department should be instructed to consider entirely new or modified ways of marketing the company's various products, with perhaps special emphasis on a certain single product or a cluster of products at a time. It should be told not to hesitate to entertain any possible course of action, no matter how radically it departs from the present. It should be free to consider ways in which the existing product might be altered, distribution channels modified or eliminated, or whatever. In short, its authorization should be extravagantly permissive by normal business standards.

In time the group would develop detailed plans for actual field-testing of new marketing schemes. In this respect, it must recognize that there are severe limits to how much can be proved or disproved about a suggestion simply through abstract research and 'numbers work'. Modern management has often become so dependent upon studies and briefs before it acts that it is likely to expect these as a routine matter in respect to novel new marketing suggestions. Yet the more novel the suggestion, the less reliable such briefs will be. Indeed, they are likely to be dangerously misleading. The reason is that they will be based on data that usually do not really apply to the details of the suggested scheme. And they will be founded on arguments that rely on inapplicable experiences. Thus a few years ago the conventional kind of business study of the best retail channels for distributing dress shirts would have emphasized traditional department and specialty stores. If you had interviewed consumers, that is where they would have said they would buy. But now suddenly they are buying increasingly at so-called 'discount' department stores. The world's best-executed study would have yielded wrong results because the idea of this new kind of outlet did not exist. Only actual experience taught the consumer of its availability and suitability and proved his willingness to use it.

When an idea or a programme is genuinely new, the usual type of supporting 'research' or 'study' brief will seldom be possible. When one is offered, it is likely to be full of strained reasoning and stretched data. Management must face the stubborn fact that when it comes to new ideas there are some things which no amount of paper-and-pencil research can either validate or clear up in advance. They require actual field tests, or in the suggested language of Seymour Kroll, market research manager of the Lumber and Plywood Division of Weyerhaeuser Company, they require 'experimental marketing'.

This means that, when the marketing development department seeks funds for testing some of its ideas, it has to seek them not from some existing sales operating committee, or even from the sales vice-president, but perhaps from the company's executive committee itself. Hardly any other group or single individual can afford to go out on the limb that the department may be suggesting.

The sales department's prior approval should not be required as such – not because sales is unimportant, but because it should not be put into the unfair position of having to pass on the desirability or feasibility of marketing schemes whose very mention might be viewed as a threat to or as an implied lack of confidence in the sales department.

If at the outset the department is set up as a strictly experimental staff operation, and if it is clearly understood that it is not to be a profit-making group, there is likely to be much less resistance to its ideas.

These ideas should of course be thoroughly developed on paper at the outset. After executive committee approval, they should be tested in carefully selected markets under as representative and controlled conditions as possible. The department itself – with the help of specially selected individuals from elsewhere in the company – would have full responsibility for making the tests. It would design and run the entire operation almost as a separate business, even down to having its own advertising agency. Only if and when the operation proves clearly successful would it be turned over, at the discretion of the executive committee, to the sales department for further implementation and extension.

This last step is a big one. It might involve a monumental upheaval in the company's operations. If, however, distribution costs can be cut while serving customers better, or if new markets can be efficiently opened, there can be no legitimate argument against the early and rapid implementation of the marketing plan, provided it meets reasonable profitability standards.

The Danger of Static Assumptions

But profit standards sometimes exercise a conservative drag far beyond what the market facts justify, and it is well to recognize why this is so. A good example is the supermarket revolution mentioned in Chapter 3. The resistance of the large grocery chains to the supermarket idea, even after its demonstrated success in the early 1930s, was completely justified by the profit-and-loss calculations they had made of supermarket operations. Where the calculations obviously went wrong was in their static assumptions about people's buying habits. They failed to see how the supermarket itself could modify the behaviour of the people it sought to convert into customers – that it would be able to employ new merchandising methods which would greatly change people's willingness to come long distances and to telescope their grocery buying into one or two big weekly shopping trips. In short, the calculations failed to consider how the supermarket innovation would itself change the environment within which the grocery industry would henceforth operate. By assuming the old corner-grocery-store environment, and the shopping habits it involved, the calculation yielded discouraging profit prospects.

Size and Innovation

One of the most important things to understand about marketing innovations is that, the bigger and more novel they are, the greater is their capacity to change the ingrained consumer habits to which they address themselves. And the greater that capacity, the greater is their chance of success.

This also applies to the companies which do the innovating. The bigger the company, the better are its chances of making the innovation stick. But it has become a cliché among the top executives of some giant corporations to say that a large company cannot afford to introduce vastly new innovations because it has such an enormous dollar and consumer-franchise investment in the present. In short, it has too much to lose.

This kind of self-restricting rhetoric in part accounts for the fact that so many successful ideas in recent years originated in, or were first exploited by, the midget fringe of American business enterprise. Some product examples are semiconductors and diodes, aerosol-spray packaging, ultrasonics, compact and small automobiles, ceramic industrial equipment, sixty-second self-developing photographic film, rocket fuels, all-purpose liquid household detergents, and frozen foods. Some examples of marketing institutions are rack jobbers, food and soft-goods supermarkets, discount houses, motels, drive-in restaurants, drive-in banks, fast-service multipump gasoline stations, specialty muffler shops, and vending-machine stores.

In self-defence, the large companies will cite Du Pont's massive and costly attack on the chemistry of polymerization, with its consequent yield of commercial nylon. But the well-known facts are that large companies have a pathological tendency to play it safe, especially when it comes to fundamental new marketing institutions. In part this is the result of size as such.

The Dangers of 'Professional Management'

The larger the company, the more screening an idea gets. This almost invariably results in screening into extinction ideas which cannot easily be proved out in advance with pencil and paper, that is, ideas which must, to a considerable extent, be accepted on faith and then tested out in actual operating situations. But the larger the company, the more it is likely to think in severely 'professional management' terms. This means that radical new ideas have to be elaborately supported by feasibility studies, and then they must wend their laborious way tortuously upward through successive committee layers before coming up for final approval. This is almost invariably a strangling process which kills off all but the most obvious and least risky propositions.

Just in new product ideas alone, where feasibility is much more easily demonstrated than in new marketing institutions or methods, the mortality rate of this kind of repetitive screening is terrific. In 1959, H. C. Buell, marketing vice-president of P. R. Mallory and Co, Inc, reported to the National Industrial Conference Board the results of a new products survey he made of 91 large industrial firms representing many industries. He found that only a fraction of the proposed new product ideas ever reached any formal screening stage, and of those screened annually and then selected for further study, there were still fewer. Thus among electronics companies, 59 were screened, 14 selected for further study; basic materials – 26 screened, 5 selected; chemicals – 40 screened, 7 selected; business equipment – 95 screened, 7 selected; and industrial products – 79 screened, 17 selected.

In the small companies there is less formalization of the management process. Responsible high executives are brought in earlier on new idea discussions. Hence they have greater access to novel suggestions than their colleagues in large companies. They may not move faster on novel new ideas, but they undoubtedly are exposed to more of them and seem therefore to back more. The mere fact that they are exposed to novelty more frequently conditions them to treat new ideas with greater receptiveness. When you constantly get a lot of odd notions brought before you, after a while some of them don't seem so odd. When you get only an occasional one, it will certainly seem to be out in left field. It dies right there. No wonder such a disproportionately small share of revolutionizing newness comes from the most powerful and best-heeled big companies.

The Advantages of Bigness

The notion that it is more risky for such companies to innovate is completely wrong. The fact is that, the larger, the more affluent, the better known, and the more respected a company is, the better are its chances of making innovations successfully, especially revolutionizing innovations. The reason is that the giant, well-respected company has automatic public esteem. The public has great confidence in nearly everything that company does. The large company does not really have to 'sell' a new idea in the same way a small unknown one does. The idea is virtually 'sold' the moment the giant company announces it because the customer will think that, if, say, Du Pont does it, 'it must be good'. Yet few giant companies think very willingly about the customer-creating advantages of their size. On the contrary, they usually apologize for their size, engaging in all sorts of public relations programmes designed to humanize their image by pretending that they are 'just folks like your next-door neighbour'.

There is little point in being a giant unless you use your size for profit-building advantage. The pioneering of powerful new innovations that break sharply from the present is such a use of bigness. One gratifying example of the use of such power in recent years is General Motors' introduction of the rear-engine Corvair. Certainly it was less risky for GM to do it than Studebaker, even had the latter been strong and solvent at the time.

Instead of blindly following the public relations route of advertising itself as being 'just folks', the large corporation should constantly build an image of powerful customer-serving competence. It is uniquely qualified to introduce the kinds of radical innovations that small companies must risk everything to push. Large corporations must realize their unique capacity to bring automatic authority to and customer support for big new customer-oriented ideas.

But they must also recognize the organizational barriers which beset them. That is why it is so important for them to match product development departments with formal marketing development programmes.

Organizing for Marketing R & D

The marketing development department must be consciously organized primarily to conceive, develop, evaluate, and test new marketing strategies and tactics – with special emphasis on profit-building ideas that depart from historic practices and break new ground.

In short, the department's chief reason for existence is the production of detailed, fundamentally new marketing proposals and programmes the impact of which is chiefly long-run and preferably massive.

Since the very nature of 'newness' is that it deals with things that have never been done before, this means that the department is the uniquely risk-taking arm of the company. But this does not mean it is exempt from carefully studying and justifying the proposals it makes and the ideas it wants to test out. On this score it must do what is doable but without limiting its proposals to those that can be 'briefed out' with the customary pencil-and-paper thoroughness.

Future Programmes versus Current Problems

It must also be recognized that the department has to stay systematically clear of trying constantly to solve today's problems today. This would force it to work carefully within the context of today's marketing operations and hence keep it from effectively thinking beyond today. A man whose chief problem is trying to keep from starving will not make a good chef at a fancy restaurant. Instead of developing exotic new dishes, he will spend his time finding and quickly consuming the ordinary stuff that is handy. The marketing development department must resolutely avoid the ordinary stuff.

But the mere fact that the department is inevitably in the kitchen where today's brew is being cooked exposes it to today's tactical problems. It will have to deal with some of these simply because the same kitchen is inescapably the source of tomorrow's brew. The company's present organization and ways of doing things are facts of life. The marketing development department operates with those facts.

This means that the department will have to organize itself to handle two kinds of projects that deal with new ideas:

1. Fundamental new marketing innovations
2. New operating tactics and standards

But since every new undertaking in some way commits the company to a course of future action, plus the fact that the company has limited capital and many places to spend it, the department must also carefully evaluate how and where to spend it. This requires systematic investment planning, which will have to be a third type of department project responsibility.

In order to assure the effective administration of all the department's projects, responsibility for their execution should be divided in such a manner that there is no internal confusion or dilution of effort. This is best accomplished by having all 'innovation projects' under one man's supervision, all 'operating tactics and standards projects' under another man's supervision, and all 'investment evaluations' under a third person.

The department's three project areas are therefore as follows:

1. Marketing innovation projects
2. Operating tactics and standards projects
3. Marketing investment planning

Avoiding Dilution of Effort

The purpose of having a separate supervisor for each project area is to avoid the dilution that will inevitably result if the same man spreads himself across a variety of projects that are vastly different in the kinds of efforts and points of view required.

Innovation strategy and operating tactics are vastly different. Both require a great deal of imagination and hard work, but the former demands comprehensive, overall, highly integrated marketing thought and planning because it will be concerned with encompassing marketing systems that are complete in themselves. The actual operating tactics are a much more limited operation dealing with specific pieces of a going marketing setup. It concerns itself with more near-term implementations. To mix up the two is virtually to guarantee the less-than-optimum achievement of the innovation projects.

The hardest thing for a going business organization to do is to overcome the urgent demands of present problems – to skip trying quickly to solve these problems in favour of long-term strategy solutions. It is always easier and therefore more tempting to plug in short-term tactical 'solutions'. Hence to have the same person deal with tactics as with encompassing strategy is to assure the dominance of tactics and to under-optimize strategy.

The reduction of the department's overall effectiveness which will result from this dilution of strategy thinking with tactical approaches will grow worse as the dilution continues over some time. The reason is that innovation projects invariably encounter more organizational opposition than any other kind. They threaten the position of people who are responsible for managing the operations which the innovations might alter or eliminate. They face these people with the possibility that the innovators will become more honoured and therefore be promoted faster. Hence the rest of the organization will tend, in various subtle or direct ways, to resist innovators and innovations. This means that the persons responsible for innovation projects have to fight harder than most people in order to do their jobs. They virtually have to 'bleed' in order to get their jobs done.

But if their direct responsibilities encompass both the innovation projects and the more easily 'saleable' tactical projects, they are apt gradually to put their major efforts on the latter because these involve less strain and bleeding. Again, innovations suffer. Therefore, if a man's single responsibility is innovation projects, he has only one thing to fight for, only one type of project in connection with which his work is judged. He will become a purposeful and devoted advocate of things which are unlikely to get done unless they do indeed have a powerful advocate.

The Department Manager

The marketing development department will have a tough and ticklish assignment. In many cases it will have to fight for unpopular, perhaps offbeat ideas. This is the inescapable nature of its job. And that means the department's manager has to be a unique type of person. In order first of all to merit the confidence of his peers in the entire company, he has to be a strong man with lots of solid line experience in the marketing field. Otherwise they will think of him as an unrealistic dreamer who has, in effect, never met a payroll. He has to be a man with outstanding analytical skills, proved imagination, a wide range of interests, solid executive skills, and an exceptional ability to get along with others. Moreover, the top management which selects this man must think of him as outstanding material for a high executive line job in the future.

Finally, at least one of the project managers in the department should have many of the same characteristics and sponsorship as the department's manager himself. This is important for two reasons: (1) To the extent that some of the department's major innovation projects are successful in their pilot tests, somebody will have to integrate these innovations throughout the company's entire marketing organization. The best-qualified man will be one who has lived with the project from its inception and through its field test. He must come from market development. But since the company-wide implementation of the innovation is necessarily a firing-line responsibility, the man who does it should be an experienced line executive in the first place, who has the confidence of the field organization. (2) The second reason that one of the project managers should have the same characteristics and sponsorship as the department's manager is that the latter should be training his own replacement. Unless he knows that a competent replacement is in his shop, he will view his job as a dead end. If that becomes the case, he will not get the satisfaction out of his job which produces the momentum, drive, and results without which the department will be a failure to begin with.

Company Climate

There are many complicated ins and outs to establishing and running a marketing development department. But beyond this, there is the corporate attitude towards experimentation and innovation.

For many years the Stanford Research Institute has been studying the reasons why certain companies have outstanding growth records and others merely drift along at the national rate of economic growth. The major conclusions are as follows:

1. They systematically seek out, find, and reach for growth products and growth markets.

2. They characteristically have organized programmes to seek and promote new business opportunities.

3. They are consistently self-critical about the adequacy of their present operations and therefore consistently demonstrate superior competitive abilities in their present lines of business.

4. Their top management slots are staffed by uniquely courageous, adventurous, high-spirited executives who bubble with dissatisfaction and are driven by an energetic zeal to lead rather than to follow.

5. The companies almost invariably have established formal systems of discovering opportunities and offsetting extreme risks by 'planning for the unseeable' within the context of

clearly defined and growth-inspiring statements of 'company goals'.

6. The chief executives consciously and continuously, by word and by deed, establish an organizational environment of ruthless self-examination and effervescent high adventure.

Top management must see that the entire company becomes saturated with the idea of creativity and the merits of self-criticism. It must develop and transmit some guiding philosophy about the creative function – indeed, the creative necessity – of the really effective business enterprise.

It is in marketing that some of the greatest cost-reducing efficiency-promoting business opportunities now lie. The reason in part is that this area has been so long neglected. Every firm, particularly the larger firm, is an active agent of the economic environment it functions in. It can help to create the kind of competitive conditions it will face in the future. And it can do a great deal to modify and create the environmental conditions which will make its products and its marketing schemes acceptable and saleable.

Most well-managed companies recognize this when it comes to products and to capital budgeting. They try to shape their own competitive futures by lavishly supporting product R & D and carefully planning long-term capital investment. It is time that they gave the same kind of support to carefully systematic R & D in marketing methods and tactics. This will enable them to shape the environmental conditions in which they will operate in the future rather than being wholly at the mercy of evolving conditions produced by the random course of events.

The most outstanding recent example of the capacity of one or two companies to shape profitably the future environment in which they will operate is the bowling-equipment industry whose remarkably successful approach was described in Chapter 2. What the automatic-pinsetter manufacturers did to sell their product was, in effect, to use it as a device to change the environment in which it was to be used. It was the changed environment, not the greater efficiency of the automatic pinsetter, which made automatic pinsetting and bowling the booming business they have become.

Creating the Future

The company that is really oriented to really big profit and big growth will not be satisfied merely with keeping in sufficiently flexible shape so that it can jump in the right direction when the competitive innovations of the future descend on it some fateful day. It must help to create the future – resolutely dedicating itself to assuming the risks (and reaping the profits) of leadership.

It must enthusiastically put itself into the business of leadership, of forcing competitors to submit to the creative profit-building marketing ideas *it* implements, rather than merely submitting to what others have dreamed up. It must recognize the value of audacity and daring. It must create within the organization a restlessly creative discontent with the here and now. Product R & D typically thinks and acts this way. And the results have been that, as a nation, we are now experiencing the most prodigious outpouring of genuinely customer-serving product newness in the history of man.

The painful parallel is that this newness has not been matched by equally customer-serving, profit-building newness in product marketing. On this score we are hardly out of the middle ages. One reason is that we are simply not being as systematically innovation-minded in marketing as we are in products. While product innovations are the result of a systematic and carefully coddled search, marketing innovations are the unsolicited, unplanned, accidental, and often the gratuitous by-products of antecedent and facilitating product development. What is needed is some serious, systematic, full-time marketing R & D. And to get it requires a separate marketing development department.

To expect the same results by merely encouraging or pushing the present marketing setup to produce them is to expect too much. It is both unrealistic and unfair. The present marketing organization has other pressing current problems, and it cannot fairly be expected to produce really good new proposals which undermine the security and self-confidence of the people responsible for making the present setup work.

9

COMMERCIAL RESEARCH AND MANAGEMENT RESPONSIBILITIES

THE PREVIOUS chapters have proposed the establishment of uniquely specialized staff groups or task forces to help management plan ahead better and to develop more effective marketing operations.

Many large corporations already have market or commercial research departments which in part could do, and in some cases will claim to do, some of the things I have suggested. Actually they seldom do it. Partly this is due to design: nobody has asked them to do it; they seldom have time to do it; and when they try to do it, they often get told to lay off. There are usually more pressing day-to-day questions that need answering and problems that need solving.

With the growing popularity of corporate long-range planning departments, a second organizational centre has been created which is cabable of some of the things I have been proposing. But the assignments of such departments are usually much more limited than what I propose, though they need not be. Corporate planning departments usually deal with two kinds of matters: (1) short- and long-term capital budgeting, and (2) a variety of specific studies such as buy-out and merger proposals, plant location studies, sometimes sophisticated logistical analyses, and so forth. Though long-term capital budgeting lends itself to raising questions about the future configuration of the society and the economy in which the company will have to operate, what usually happens is that these studies simply confine themselves to making elaborate statistical projections of current trends. There is seldom any serious study of or accounting for the many external factors which might drastically affect the slopes and directions of these trends.

This does not mean that corporate planning departments are staffed by shortsighted and inadequate people. Far from it. They are often among the most obviously capable staff personnel in the entire company. The trouble is not with their brains or perception but with management's expectations. Management usually demands what it calls 'solid' and 'verifiable' facts. This means mammoth studies and reports full of awesomely reliable-looking statistics, charts, graphs, rate-of-return calculations, discounted cash flow ratios, and the like. Management demands and gets these because that is what it established the planning department for – to stop relying on vague hopes and crude guesses about the future and get down to some solid studies and numbers.

The result is that, although many companies believe they are getting sound long-range thinking, they are only getting the kind of important but incomplete (and sometimes spurious) planning they have specifically forced their staffs to confine themselves to. But even if these staffs were franchised to do something more, it is doubtful that they could provide the sort of things suggested earlier. The reason is, as already pointed out, that this takes specialized talents and some sort of separate organizational status.

Some of these talents are often available in the market research department. But as a general proposition, it is useless to expect from the department itself any of the things I have outlined. Some distressing and dangerous things have happened in market research in recent years which seriously affect its utility for much of anything. In view of its galloping ascendance, it is time management gave some tough thought to the proper role and operation of market research in the modern corporation.

The Ascendance of Commercial Research

The market researcher, the psychological and motivation researcher, the sales analyst and planner, and the economist are in business to stay. They form an élite corps of corporate functionaries on whose findings and recommendations top management increasingly relies. The question is: How good a job does commercial research do? Can it be relied upon? Should it be improved? Can it be?

The vaunted values of commercial research have been praised with lofty self-seriousness by its dedicated practitioners. For a line executive today to express some misgivings about its usefulness is to mark him as a philistinic reactionary who should be ridiculed into silence. The usual tactic is to call him some sort of 'old-school' mossback who is to be pitied more than scorned. He simply doesn't know the score. He doesn't understand what market research really is and does.

But the fact is that there is an enormous gulf between what business and professional journals and textbooks say commercial research can do for business and what it so often succeeds in doing. As in all fields, aspiration does not assure realization. There's something missing somewhere.

The Missing Ingredients of Commercial Research

Actually there are two things missing. One is that market researchers often lack a fully developed sense of responsibility regarding the meanings of their findings; the other is that they lack imaginative audacity.

Market researchers talk often, long, and persuasively about the indispensable necessity and values of research. But when they issue their elaborate reports, one seldom finds any solid action-oriented policy suggestions on the basis of which management might get a more certain feeling that market research is indeed necessary and useful. In short, market researchers seldom accept any responsibility for explaining in detail why their studies came out the way they did – why, for example, market share declined, and what the company might do to improve its position. The research is irresponsible about its findings.

The second missing ingredient in so much of today's commercial research is imaginative audacity. Too often commercial research has become too formalized with statistical method and too ritualized with scientific pretences. Moreover, in picking commercial researchers, management is often too preoccupied with getting personable team-workers –

sound, level-headed, feet on the ground, cooperative, and clean-cut. In short, dull. The process of natural selection turns too many commercial research departments into elaborate machines single-mindedly devoted to the ceremonial reiteration of the commonplace.

Under these circumstances even a brilliant researcher may be engulfed in what becomes a sea of mediocrity, soaking it up as bread soaks up gravy. But more commonly he simply doesn't get hired in the first place. Usually he ends up in the more permissive society of a good university, as the inside man in some go-getting consulting organization, or in an advertising agency. The typical operating corporation either doesn't hire him, forces him out after he sees what the score is, or transforms him into the dull counterpart of those who hired him. After a while, a merely fair job of analysis or run-of-the-mill ideas get labelled as being exceptional because mediocrity has become a norm which passes for quality. Management never really learns about the dramatic potentials of commercial research. It erroneously thinks that what it is getting exhausts what is possible.

But saying that management has only itself to blame may overstate things a bit. The researchers themselves are far from innocent. They usually visualize their function too narrowly. They consider 'insight' to consist of and end with defining the problem and designing and using a statistical research apparatus with which to tackle it. Huge quantities of data are collected, sorted, sifted, arrayed, manipulated, averaged, tabled, charted, and finally disgorged in an orgiastic consumption of time and money. What emerges is an elaborately dolled up report designed to create an aura of unassailable and incontrovertible fact – repetitious, routine, and prosaic though it is. Even when the results are new, they are likely to *look* old because they are presented in a dull businessese or in a sort of anaemic popularization of professional jargon.

The Failures of Commercial Research

Commercial research is today presumed to teach line executives better to know the market, the customer, the economy, and the future than they were able to know in the old days of rules of thumb, feel of the market, inspiration, hunch, and prophetic insight. With the help of commercial research management is supposed to be able to know more, think straighter, plan better, and risk less. Much of this presumed value of commercial research is achieved, and management is often profusely grateful.

But there is another side to the coin – a very unedifying side. The unhappy fact is that, while it perhaps clarifies much and helps greatly, commercial research often unintentionally covers up more. Under the statistics, and in the name of systematic, scientific analysis and presentation of its findings, there lies the smothered, vibrant creativeness and spark to which the company could be pushed if things were done differently.

In other words, there is a serious question of whether commercial research may not in many cases actually be sucking much of the vital force out of a company by the very process of its thoughtful, scientific, analytical approach to business problems and issues. The totemic process of dignifying forecasts and problem solving with elaborate surveys, studies, and statistical manipulations may be, as Professor John Jeuck has suggested, more of a millstone than a milestone. To the extent that the more so-called 'professional managers' unfailingly require a market study before any significant move is made, they may be submitting the entire process of business policy making into a dreary procrustean mould which automatically precludes suggestions and ideas that are not directly or easily measurable or statistically verifiable. If the rules of scientific management require that action be preceded by study, and if 'study' is interpreted to mean statistical facts and surveys, then anything which cannot be easily measured before the fact will not get done. That would be 'flying by the seat of your pants', and in much of today's professional rhetoric this is a cardinal taboo.

Hence the method of science, instead of being a glorious liberator, may actually be a deadening confiner. Instead of encouraging new, dramatic, inspiring, provocative ideas and opening new doors of opportunities, it may discourage ideas and close doors. If an idea does not appear to be quantifiable in some way or immediately capable of objective testing, it is not likely to get a hearing. To the extent that management insists on this kind of 'full documentation', the pretences of 'scientific management' are their own worst enemy.

But commercial research is certainly no innocent bystander, merely doing what it is told. It too is out to cultivate a suitable professional reputation for scientific dignity and level-headed probity. Hence it often limits itself to doing what is clearly respectable and easily defensible.

The very presence in the company of a group that never permits itself to make a proposal or a judgement without first making a detailed study tends to establish throughout the company the pseudoscientific principle that one measure of a proposal's respectability is that it must be verifiable and testable on paper. Hence the commercial research department may exercise a disproportionately restrictive influence on the whole company. It may keep others in the organization from the kind of venturesome, audacious, provocative thinking which cuts through convention, prescription, and routine – the very attitude which characterizes protean innovationist thinking at its best.

The Function of Expertness

Commercial researchers provide important business services. Nobody in his right mind suggests anything different. But the point is to get commercial research to function at its useful best. This means researchers must be more than merely good craftsmen. They must be innovationists both in research methods and in practical commercial ideas. Above all, they must make their professional expertness produce meaningful, usable results rather than employing it merely as a shield against facing up to solid responsibility.

What does this mean and what does it involve?

First, it involves knowing what expertness is for. Expertness encompasses much more than the elaboration and use of formal techniques in research and analysis. More than anything else it should be viewed as involving imaginative audacity in the interpretation of data and events and in formulating positive action-oriented proposals for management's consideration.

Imaginative expertness has a special licence. It does not have to document and prove everything it says. It has the right to cut through the mountainous accumulation of data and to bypass the sinuous analytical maze of respectable methodology in order swiftly and decisively to reach findings and suggest actions. Without that right the expert gets no credit for his expertness and his employer no extra benefit from his specialized skills. If every time he speaks he has to lay a stack of detailed analytical materials on the table in order to substantiate every comment, he is a mere technician, not an expert. An expert is somebody who has earned the right to speak up without necessarily putting up.

Staff expertness must function as it is intended to function. If an expert is going to confine himself to what is clearly provable, if he is going to play it safe by clinging dependently to his data, nobody will get any benefit from his expertness. Expertness must cut through and around facts. It must imagine what the facts do not clearly encompass. It must begin where the clearly verifiable ends.

This is what the old-time business entrepreneur did before the advent of professionalized commercial research and the fetishes of scientific management. He went on hunches and on feel for the situation. He extended his imagination to the perception of the presently improbable and the expectation of the presently unanticipated. That is what Robert E. Wood did shortly after the First World War when, as a young executive at Montgomery Ward, he wrote a long memorandum urging the company to shift its emphasis away from mail-order sales by establishing a chain of retail stores. This memorandum, which Ward executive Howard H. Green recently unearthed from forgotten files, is one of the great prophetic documents of American business history. Except for its slight reference to fragmentary census data and its sketchy analysis of the costs and probable return of such a switch, it is entirely devoid of statistics. Its heart and power lie in pure skill of perception regarding the changing nature of American society. Wood was unable to persuade Ward's top management. He quit and took his ideas to Julius Rosenwald of Sears, Roebuck and Company, where their merits and Wood's personal merits were quickly recognized. Wood went on to Sears to implement them with vigour and singular success, to Ward's everlasting pain.

Of course, the old-time executive was often forced to act almost completely on hunch and feel because he had so little data. As the result, he was often grievously wrong. Now, with more data, the trick is to become the master of data, not their slave. Data tell nothing, only people do. Data must be interpreted. But even interpretation is not enough. Data must be used creatively and imaginatively. For the commercial researcher this imposes the inescapable necessity to get to know the entire spectrum of business activities better, to understand better and more sympathetically the problems of line management, and to recognize the essential importance of innovation in business success.

The triumph of certain data merchants in commercial research too often inhibits creative and imaginative effort. Too often nothing is permissible in the way of making policy or entertaining ideas unless the data are so unambiguously in favour of proposed policies or ideas that even the elevator operator can see their merit. Such rigid standards can be fatal. To wait until the data clearly tell what should be done is to wait until they're so overwhelmingly suggestive as to what course to follow that it is too late. Competitors will already have acted. Change should be made before the fact that it is imminent materializes to the point of competitors or conditions having already taken their toll.

The only time data speak so clearly that everybody easily gets the point is when it is too late. Then they speak not with a gentle whisper or a subtle hint but with a devastating and perhaps mortal blast.

The older management dependence on hunch, inspiration, and self-confident pushing is by today's standard a quack approach to decision making. But today's approach is all too often quack in its own elevated way. Where the older method was often like metaphysics, today's is often like pseudoscience. The worse of the two is the latter because pseudoscience has a nasty way of becoming a prescription for inaction. Science makes and tests hypotheses; that is, it makes suggestions designed ultimately to explain phenomena, behaviour, or operations. Above all, it is open-minded and experimental. Too often commercial research is just the opposite. Instead of opening doors it closes them. If every statement must be quantifiably verified – if that is what science pretends to be – it becomes a triumphant inhibitor of the unusual and the imaginative. If it is the censor of offbeat ideas and suggestions, if it permits the emergence only of the routine statistics that are reducible to the calculating machine – if it does this, it is a sorry day for the dramatic innovationism that characterizes a creative society.

There are lots of situations in business today where what passes for innovation is only a process of fringe adaptation to marginal adjustments that result from small ideas and lesser inspirations. In practically everything they do, most firms are little more than drifting with events. They have not learned the commercial importance of being active agents of their environment – that they are more than merely a part of it. They help create it. The firm that does not constantly try to change itself and its environment becomes vulnerable to the changes made by others.

Entrepreneurship versus Research

Two of the most profound examples of how, through sheer entrepreneurial brilliance, even small companies in their industries can greatly change the environment in which they operate and thus enormously benefit themselves are provided by the Columbia Recording Corporation's 50 per cent price reduction of its classical records in the summer of 1940 and by American Motors' pioneering development of a market for compact cars in the 1950s. Perhaps the most significant thing about both these enormously successful operations was that the usual kinds of routine commercial research clearly advised against them.

Columbia at the time had only a fraction of the classical records market, with Victor the dominant firm by far. Although Columbia was making money on its current classical sales, it had to more than double them in order to break even with its proposed price reduction. It also knew that such a cut would encounter dealer difficulties since their dollar margins per record would be reduced. Hence dealers would tend to steer customers to competitive records. Furthermore, Columbia realized that discriminating record buyers would tend to avoid low-priced recordings on the assumption that they must be inferior. Finally, Columbia saw that, if buyers did shift to the lower-priced recordings in any significant number, Victor would meet the lower price, and Columbia's advantage would be dissipated.

What, then, was the sense of cutting prices? Mr Edward Wallerstein, Columbia's new president, believed that at the much-reduced price the total industry demand for classical records would expand greatly. This would enable Columbia to grow much faster than at its then satisfactory rate. But commercial research could not possibly have verified that the market could be greatly expanded. The serious collectors of records, who accounted for the predominant proportion of classical record sales, were currently buying the most costly brands featuring the best-known performers. No amount of interviewing would have suggested that they might buy lower-priced brands. But Wallerstein had noticed with extreme interest that a recent circulation promotion by a New York newspaper which offered classical albums at prices averaging a third of Columbia's pre-reduction price sold more than 50,000 sets of a single symphony in a few weeks when the average sales of a classical album over a two-year period were between 6,000 and 10,000. Later he noted that the National Committee for Music Appreciation, offering a series of twelve symphonies at prices under a third of the major company prices, was achieving enormous sales without showing either the names of the orchestras or the conductors and without enabling customers to play the records before buying them.

From these fragmentary developments Mr Wallerstein concluded that there was great interest in classical music among relatively unsophisticated music listeners. Certainly a sophisticated listener would not have bought an unknown brand, with unknown performers, and without advance sampling. And he would probably not have bought at these depressed prices because of his suspicion that 'you get what you pay for'. Wallerstein concluded that there was a big untapped market for low-priced classical records. If they were also quality records with known performers, he felt that the market among sophisticated collectors would probably also expand.

With this in mind, for two years he quietly improved the physical quality of his records and developed a large stable of well-known artists and orchestras. His constant plan was not just to do a better job of what everybody else was doing and thereby capture a greater market share but to change the market itself by doing what his competitors were *not* doing. He planned to change the external conditions which faced his company, not just by appealing more effectively to existing classical record customers, but by *creating entirely new customers*. He intended greatly to expand the market. When his price cut came, Victor and others followed suit three days later. And everybody greatly benefited. The total market expanded just as Wallerstein had supected.

As I have indicated, the usual methods of consumer research could not possibly have either discovered the possibilities which Mr Wallerstein suspected or validated his suspicions. If anything, researchers would have argued powerfully against his proposal simply because research could not have provided sufficient certainty about the possibilities of an expansible market to convince the researchers themselves. And certainly no self-respecting professional manager would have been convinced.

The same thing was obviously true of compact cars in the early stages of American Motors' thinking about this new product. Mr George Romney, American Motors' president, somehow felt that a market could be created. But he knew that it took a special kind of sales-promoting zeal to do it. For this he was uniquely qualified because of his Mormon missionary experience as an evangelical speaker. He single-handedly created the market by personally addressing thousands of women's clubs and business meetings and passionately declaring the legitimacy of compact-car ownership, the idiocy of big-car expense, and the needlessness of big-car in-town inconvenience. Meanwhile, Detroit's 'Big Three', with armies of market researchers to guide them, sat idle while Rambler miraculously pushed into third place in the 1959–60 model year.

The Responsibilities of Research

Today in business there is no such thing as respectability's coming to the firm that preserves the glories and pretences of the past. This merely incubates organizational inertia and debilitation. The company's metabolism counts this debilitation with unerring accuracy, even if its management does not.

But what business is all this of commercial research? It is everything, because one of its minimal functions is to keep track of the company's metabolism. Its duty is not only to know what is happening to the company but also to prescribe what should be done to achieve what ought to be happening. This again requires imaginative audacity. It means chucking the paralysing opiate that staff work is staff work and line work is line work and never the twain shall meet. Staff work conceived this narrowly is *irresponsible*. Unless it has a sense of responsibility for what happens, it will not view its task as encompassing anything more than simple data collection and processing. This is a prescription for intellectual and imaginative sterility. For if staff has no responsibility for what happens to the company, staff work cannot be expected to have the kind of strident zeal which breeds ideas, inspirations, suggestions, and imaginative applications of know-how.

One function of top management, then, is to make staff departments responsible for what happens to the company. But responsibility without authority is useless. Management must do one more thing. It must give the direct head of the commercial research department top management status. If the company has a largely 'inside' board of directors, he should be a member. If it has a largely 'outside' board, he should be on the highest policy committees. If commercial research is to be made responsible, it must know what is going on in the highest policy circles, and it must have direct opportunity and authority to influence high policy. If management gives commercial research this role and these responsibilities, it will force it to go beyond simple data analysis and into policy considerations that require constant alertness to the possibilities suggested by creative interpretations of commercial data.

Thus when the market researchers repeatedly produce figures showing a declining market position, they should be held responsible and hold themselves responsible for explaining why. But beyond that, they should be responsible for suggesting ways to turn the tide. They cannot be permitted the easy luxury of saying that this is 'the sales department's job' or 'line management's job'. A company cannot allow an atmosphere in which commercial research personnel, viewing the statistics they turn out, merely sit on the sidelines lamenting the failure of the top brass to 'do something'. It is staff's own uncompromising duty to 'do something'; to find out what is wrong and what is right and to assume the responsibility for suggesting remedies – and to do all this without special management prodding.

When it comes to actual forecasting, and particularly to long-range forecasting, staff's responsibility assumes another dimension. The usual building-block technique of basing future estimates on simple projections of population growth, consumption rates, man-hours of employment, per-worker productivity, etc. – that is, on the extension of present rates of change of particular variables – these are clearly not enough. They have the simple merit of statistical meaningfulness. But they lack the more complex and difficult quality of judgement. They lack vision and spontaneity. They lack the most important component of all : prophetic imagination.

What Management Wants

There is a strong preference among practical-minded business managers for the notion that proposed policies and ideas should make sense in terms of the managers' own direct experiences and that they should fit neatly into the present scheme of corporate policies and practices. Management is sceptical about things involving unusual departures in methods of analysis, exposition of results, and policy implications. But few really good ideas are so obviously good that they achieve immediate acclaim. They have to be fought for. This fact alone should be viewed by their originators as making them worth fighting for. Even if their value lies only in stirring up the placid contentment that encrusts so many companies, they often serve an important function.

The commercial research staff is in the unusual position of having time, or being able to make time, to study problems and trends without the burden of solving a multitude of daily operating problems. Commercial research staffs must view themselves as being in part responsible for what their statistics show. If the statistics have turned bad, they must find out why, no matter what their assigned duties, and recommend what should be done about it.

It is at this stage that the functions and limitations of statistics must be clearly understood. Statistics must not be permitted to confine recommendations to what statistics can clearly prove or support. They must be viewed as catalysing staff's imagination. Social facts must be viewed as providing guideposts to drifts of change. And the analyst's expertness must be viewed as bringing to these data the responsibility to cultivate audacious insights where grovelling research cannot perform adequately or takes too long to perform at all. In short, commercial research must view itself as being responsible for what the statistics show and should show. Its responsibilities must encompass the duty to act courageously. Expertness must be viewed as involving the right to say what cannot be immediately proved and to say it with flair and forthrightness. Indeed, without flair and forthrightness ideas too often fail to catch on, even when merit is clearly on their side.

Staff researchers often complain that management will ignore a suggestion they have been making for years but quickly adopt it when an outside consultant says the same thing. The usual implication is that management does not listen to its own staff.

But the facts are usually quite the opposite. To be sure, an outsider tends to get a better hearing simply because he is a specialist specifically called in to do an urgent job. But frequently he is more successful because of *how* he says things, not because of what he says. The reason he is a successful consultant is not always because he is brighter than other people, but because he says things in a more convincing fashion. One of the occupational hazards which afflict many commercial research departments is a fatal dullness in personal expression and data presentation. Their reports read as if they were translated from German. Their personal face-to-face discussions with top management are a painful mixture of ponderous academic prose and ambiguous businessese. Their argument is full of involuted qualifications and 'if's, 'and's, and 'but's. It lacks simple directness; but most of all it lacks self-assured forthrightness. Instead of making top management's job easier with clean, brief, and precise statements and analyses, it makes its job tougher by parading before it a lot of troublesome doubts and unnecessary qualifications.

Top management wants to know the facts, which obviously include the 'if's, 'and's, and 'but's. But it also wants, needs, and has a right to expect findings and recommendations that sweep away all but the most essential of these qualifications. The researcher must know, as the effective consultant does, that what management ultimately must do is to act. The researcher's responsibility is to help him act. He must make specific alternative suggestions based on his evaluation of the importance of the 'if's, 'and's, and 'but's, not leave it up to management to do that trying job by itself.

If my prescription that the researcher should act the expert that he ought to be, that he ought to say what he believes even if it cannot be immediately proved with facts and figures, and that he ought to speak forthrightly and without doubt-creating equivocation – if this sounds like the obsolete technique of the hard-boiled, desk-pounding tycoon of yesterday, that is in part exactly what is intended. The difference is that the expert researcher is presumed to have built a pretty solid professional foundation for what he says and believes, even though the foundation may not always be easily demonstrable.

Having articulated the imaginative, research can then be directed to its study. But in no case should a very proper respect for the objectifiable become a hindrance to imagination or the sole arbiter of what is to be done. There must be a wider tolerance for the unusual personality and imaginative technician to make his own rules in commercial research. Management's job is not only to hire and encourage such a man; it must above all make the staff responsible for what the statistics show in order to force it to be more searching, more daring, and more imaginative.

The Forms and Limits of Responsibility

There are, of course, limits beyond which it is silly to hold staff responsible for what operating statistics show. Actually, there must be shared responsibility at all levels of management and in all company functions. But one thing for which nobody can be held responsible is what happens to the economy as a whole. For example, if the economist predicts that gross national product will grow by 4 per cent each quarter during the coming year, he cannot be responsible for its going down the fourth quarter. What might be done, however, is to make him accountable for his error, even if all other economists in the country were similarly wrong. This is one of the things that is badly needed: a hard-boiled post-mortem of economic and sales forecasts. Too many corporate forecasters get away with mistakes too easily. Management cannot get along without forecasters, but this does not justify complete freedom from accountability for their mistakes.

This management indulgence of forecast error is especially surprising, and even reprehensible, in view of the great emphasis that corporate forecasters put on statistics and statistical methods. The statistics convey an air of scientific reliability. That is often part of the forecaster's pseudo-scientific art. So much the more reason he should be required to explain when his science yields wrong answers.

The elaborate scientification of forecasting is another symptom of the failure of expertness which has been mentioned above. When forecasts are cast in the rigid mould of science, while the scientific requirement of controlled variables cannot possibly be fulfilled, the results are bound to be anaemic, even if correct. There being no allowance for wisdom, intuition, and hunch – the ingredients which must take over when science has no more to say – the job is only half done. If the expert can only say what the figures say, there is no need for an expert, only a technician. The fact is that in all the sciences, and especially the social sciences, the experts with the best records have always dared to go beyond formal statistics. They have been successful because their most important tool has been prophetic insight.

The point of all this is that again there is room for more imaginative treatment of commercial research, with the emphasis on doing more than the statistics permit, emphasizing what expertness is supposed to do with imagination, and holding research responsible for what its studies show.

No one argues with the increasing use and utility of statistics. Indeed, one really serious trouble in many corporate commercial research departments is the failure to keep up with the more difficult and involuted statistical and mathematical techniques being developed elsewhere. The problem unfortunately is that these methods have all too often resulted in the expert shirking his duty to speak when facts and statistics do not or cannot verify. The result has been the deadening of imagination, the extinction of spirit, and the abdication of serious responsibility for what the statistics show. But in this case it is well to recognize that the fault lies not with statistical methods but with statistical practitioners.

And in part the delinquency of the practitioners in this respect is due to the fact that line management often does not really want an imaginative and self-confidently vigorous research staff, with its possibilities for raising embarrassing questions and pointing accusing fingers. When management does not want vindication of opinions already formed, judgements already made, and steps already taken, it often passes the buck of its own responsibilities by asking commercial research to produce ungetable facts that will tell management exactly what to do about certain specific problems.

On this score, Clarence B. Randall, former board chairman of the Inland Steel Company, has laid much of the failure of commercial research squarely on management's own doorstep. He says that management simply wants too much – wants research to solve problems and produce answers that only management itself can solve. He says that:[1]

> The timorous and hard-pressed executive, who deep down inside resents and resists change ... seeks refuge in statistics. Not sure of his own thinking and hesitant to plunge boldly ahead on a plan of his own that would put his personal status in hazard, he takes protective covering in conformity with whatever general level of conduct seems to be emerging. ... His first step is to order a survey. He does this under the plausible pretext that he must ascertain the facts before reaching a decision, but actually be is seeking reassurance drawn from the law of averages. It is both easier and safer to follow the rest. And since many of the rest will be behaving exactly the same way, a colourless format of unimaginative uniformity can envelop an entire segment of our economy, solely for lack of leaders who have the courage to dig beneath the statistics and evaluate the imponderables.

Commercial research cannot produce absolutely perfect information that points unambiguously to a given course of action. Anybody who says it can is overselling the commodity. All it can do is provide perhaps better informational raw material and some suggestions based on its findings. From

[1] Clarence B. Randall, 'The Myth of the Magic Numbers', *Dun's Review & Modern Industry*, March 1961, p. 34.

there on management is on its own, doing what it gets paid so much more than staff for doing, that is, making decisions on the basis of incomplete information. That is what management is all about – taking risks. For it to insist on information that will clearly 'tell us what to do' is to demand a spurious exactness. In effect it involves abdication of management responsibility.

Regrettably, the insistence on tell-us-what-to-do type of information is becoming more common. Transfixed by the emancipating possibilities of commercial research, management increasingly withdraws into a protective integument of staff reports, turned out by people who have become conditioned to saying the commonplace and the innocuous – in short, to not rocking the boat. Under these circumstances it is hardly surprising that so many companies seldom ever get off dead centre, that the snail's pace is the typical pace even in some of our supposedly dynamic companies.

10

COMMUNICATIONS BOTTLENECKS IN PRODUCT POLICY AND ADVERTISING

THERE IS a second aspect of commercial research which is threatening sales-building originality, particularly in product policy and advertising. This is management's often uncritical reliance on consumer and motivation research. While the researchers must take much of the blame for the things which are going wrong, the real source of the trouble is not so much the technicians who produce the research as the executives who use it. That is the inescapable conclusion one draws from some very remarkable things that have been happening recently.

Nearly everyone now agrees that consumer research is a powerful management tool. Its liberating efficacy is widely proclaimed. It is said to help free the decision maker from the terrible anxieties which beset earlier generations of executives who were forced to decide on the basis of hunches, a feel for the market, or sometimes just the rawest kind of blind guessing. Decisions can now be made in a more factual and scientific context. Particularly in the case of motivation research (or M-R) has management gone into a tribal snake dance – everyone is following everyone else; and the glee is unconfined.

Proofless Pudding

But how useful is the research which is passed on to executives? More important, how good are the decisions they now make? One indication is what has happened in three industries where consumer and motivation research have made as much progress as they have anywhere. The specific products that I have in mind are (1) the new general-purpose liquid cleaners, (2) mentholated cigarettes, and (3) compact cars. The remarkable similarity of what has happened with each of these products in recent years raises serious questions about the way management is using and relying on motivation and consumer research.

Liquid Cleaners. On the heels of Lestoil's remarkable success, the nation's three soap giants launched their own brands of liquid cleaners. They were Lever Brothers' 'Handy Andy', Procter & Gamble's 'Mr Clean', and Colgate's luckless 'Genie'. They made their belated debuts within about a year of one another. Each of their names, containers, and copy themes was carefully evaluated from every possible angle by the best talent available. The result: a senseless sameness that violates some very elementary rules of marketing.

Each brand started out radiating extreme masculine symbolism that combined powerful phallic overtones with magical connotations. Each used advertising art and copy themes of a puissant wonder-worker suggesting muscular virility and transcendent potency. Even the bottles had a deliberately suggestive hand-fitting gripability. The entire effort was an integrated extension and embellishment of an obsessive preoccupation with the housewife's presumably tropistic preference for magical masculine prowess.

Menthol Cigarettes. The prodigality of new mentholated cigarettes makes the typical cigarette counter smell like an Oriental tearoom. Here is another greatly researched product and package. Entire market research teams owe their existence to the beneficial largess of tobacco companies. After many elaborately intricate consumer interviews and colour-preference tests, the researchers concluded in chorus that green suggests freshness, coolness, probably youthful idealism, and half a dozen other tranquillizing images that endear the smoker to a mentholated cigarette. The result is that every new menthol brand was wrapped in a turquoise froth of luxuriant flora, majestic waterfalls, or verdant holiday ribbon. Yet nothing could be better contrived to violate the elementary rules of selling.

Here is a product that everyone knows involves a lot of impulse brand selection. That is why cigarette marketers have always tried to create a mesmeric advertising ditty that sticks firmly in people's minds. Instead of encouraging the customer to make a careful brand choice, the strategy has usually been to send him into a hypnotic trance so that he will automatically 'Sound off for Chesterfield' or 'Call for Philip Morris'. That is also why cigarette advertising has produced so many popular clichés. Hence we have, in addition to the above, 'I'd walk a mile for a Camel', 'L.S.–M.F.T.', 'They satisfy', 'Winston tastes good like a cigarette should', and 'Filter, Flavor, flip-top box'.

Cigarette and advertising executives have always recognized that, where impulse buying is important and where one brand is virtually interchangeable with another, you have to distinguish the brands by making the packages look different and the advertising say different things. But these obvious truths are now being scuttled. Whereas each of the new menthol packages *should* have tried to achieve sales-promoting distinctiveness, they buried themselves, instead, in a green sea of indistinguishable sameness. It may be true that the green package appealed to the customer during a home interview or in a sealed, air-conditioned test room. But the endless array of green packages which confronts him at the counter makes another green package frustrating, not facilitating.

Nor does the supporting advertising copy do anything to improve matters. It actually reinforces the frustration because in every case it is carefully integrated with the brand's stubborn accentuation of the same opaque image of soft, green coolness. Instead of achieving a sales-building distinctiveness, the brands all end up in a light, cool lather of liquid similarity. The smoker is even deprived of any distinctiveness in the copy claims about the attributes of the various mentholated cigarettes. Just as the packages look the same, the claims sound the same. One possible exception up to 1962 is Alpine cigarettes, for which the findings of Elmo Roper and Color Research Institute helped produce a unique sales pitch that emphasized the direct satisfaction of specific customer needs rather than the usual unvarying emphasis on outdoor cleanliness and wholesome fun. But even here the pitch was blunted by the monotonous mellowness of Alpine's me-too mint-tinted package. And later, after a change in advertising agencies produced the even more sensible theme of legitimate masculinity ('Who put the men in Menthol? Alpine, that's who'), the theme's effectiveness continued to suffer from the package's and the point-of-sale displays' routine similarity to competing brands. With the advent of this new theme one Madison Avenue wag suggested that the next phase of Alpine's advertising merry-go-round would be the claim that 'Alpine contains ground-up men'.

What seems to have happened with menthol cigarettes is that brand distinctiveness is sacrificed to consumer research findings produced under artificial, non-market conditions. Management has translated these findings into product policies without proper regard for the competitive environment in which such policies have to operate.

Compact Cars. Here is one of the most vastly researched commodities of modern times. Detroit probably harbours the most prodigious collection of consumer information about a particular product of any single community in the entire commercial universe. Whatever one may say about its quality or intentions, in Detroit the urge towards market research is pathological. The names of the compact cars have been especially carefully researched. The letters of the alphabet were thrown together to produce name combinations by the thousands. Enormous numbers of two-syllable and one-syllable words were gathered, invented, and tested.

Finally there emerged, in the fall of 1959, three remarkably similar but competing names – Valiant, Corvair, Falcon – each of six or seven letters, two syllables, each familiar to the language, each suggesting lightness, modernness, vitality, youthfulness, strength, flight, and romantic valour.

The year before these self-same triplets made their ambiguous debut we got the Lark, a shorter, four-letter entry with the same symbolic attributes as its tardy 1959 cousins. The four-letter convention was continued early in 1960 with Dart, which was soon matched by an in-between, five-letter number called the Comet. Dart and Comet themselves inaugurated a second round of patronymic confusion. Close on their heels came the Invader, the Lancer, the Tempest, and the F-85 Rocket. With predictable continuity, all six were simple and familiar Anglo-Saxon words, all suggesting thrust, speed, strength, aggressive power, and irrepressible assertiveness. They have much the same meaning as Thunderbird. Indeed, Detroit seems to have been seized with the curious idea that an automobile brand name must have an *obvious* meaning, even if it sounds the same as its redundant competitors. Neutral or honorific appellations are out – the late lamented Edsel sealed their doom.

This is the legacy of the latest wrinkle in commercial research, finally ascendant and now firmly in the saddle, with its compulsive preoccupation with psychological imagery, social-class symbolism, and 'contemporary' values. As the result, Detroit has issued a confusing collocation of compact cars all of whose names in each price and size group sound and even look alike, with none properly distinct from the others. The only properly distinctive name in the compact field is Rambler, and it is fifty years old and was not researched even for a minute.

As in the case of liquid cleaners and menthol cigarettes, the logic and research which spawned these automobile brand names and designs were originally applied with blind and ruinous regularity in compact-car advertising. While the compact car is a deliberate departure from the big car and was baptized as America's superior version of automotive miniaturization, the accompanying advertisements quickly returned to a familiar and identical story, not of compact virtues but of big-car attributes. From the beginning, Valiant claimed the *biggest* truck in the compact field. Falcon claimed more *big-car, king-size* features than any other compact car. Lark ran full-page ads proclaiming the certain superiority of its *big* V-8 engine. And so it goes.

One begins to suspect that the compact car is a basically non-American, un-American, anti-American, a-American contrivance. Compactness must not endure. Only a few months after the compact revolution became official in 1959, the auto companies were busy canonizing the virtues of bigness and of

V-8 power, readying the unaware consumer for the longer, lower, bigger, heavier, fancier, more expensive compacts that were already in the offing.

Science or Fad?

It is more than a little disturbing to note that, in the industries and advertising agencies where consumer research has made considerable progress, products and promotional consequences are often uniformly and disastrously similar. The products, the packages, and the promotions have a dreary cookie-press sameness. It is a bitter irony that at the height of twentieth-century inventiveness, of consumer research brilliance, and of capitalist momentum, our marketing effort seems to be shrouded in a paralysis of the imagination. Why? Why are the policies of the most ardent users of consumer and motivation research so much alike? Two possible answers are worth considering:

1. Consumer research may have become so thoroughly scientific that any well-trained practitioner who studies a given problem independently of every other practitioner necessarily comes up with the same answers and the same proposed courses of action. This would account for three detergents with the same type of name, the same imagery, and the same type of container. It would account for compact cars with the same types and lengths of names and, to a lesser extent, with similar advertisements. And it would also account for our being awash in a green marsh of mentholated madness.

2. A second possible answer is imitation. First one company discovers an effective success formula, and then everybody either deliberately or unconsciously imitates it. Actually, imitation is a common practice and accounts for such TV programming fads as redundant quiz shows, ubiquitous westerns, repetitious private eyes, abundant spectaculars, and so forth. Imitation also accounts for the rapid acceptance of new clothing styles and – in women's clothes particularly – their remarkably short tenure. It accounts for best-seller fads like sexy books on advertising men and bureaucratic business infighting, movie fads about teen-age tensions, and advertising

copy fads like cigarette medical claims, filter claims, and the cyclical revival of taste and flavour claims.

Within the tight-knit fraternity of commercial researchers (motivation researchers, in particular), some say that their specialty has become so sophisticated that it produces almost identical answers to a problem studied independently by different people. But sometimes researchers produce diametrically opposed answers and solutions, as in the case of prunes. One nationally famous motivation researcher, interpreting people's attitudes and feelings, concluded that more prunes could be sold if the industry admitted and promoted their laxative qualities. Another equally famous authority concluded that more prunes could be sold if the industry avoided any laxative suggestion and emphasized, instead, their refreshing qualities.

Everybody has his own favourite example of contradictory findings being advanced by equally reputable motivational experts, or of contradictory recommendations based upon similar findings.

But if it is true, then, that motivation research is to a great extent imprecise and artless, why have independent experts produced such similar findings on detergents, cars, and cigarettes? One explanation may be that it is precisely because such research is *not* mature and *not* scientific. Perhaps the similarities result from self-conscious and worried researchers spending a great deal of time consulting and reinforcing each other. It could well be that, if they were more confident about the reliability of their work, there would be less professional consultation and greater research diversity.

Of course, professionals in all fields consult each other as a matter of routine, but there is a special reason for heavy consultation among motivation researchers. Business is using more and more of them for more and more marketing problems. This is not necessarily because executives 'believe in' motivation research, but often because they believe they cannot afford to ignore it.

Motivation researchers are a unique breed, totally different from the usual business functionary. They tend to be brilliantly imaginative, colourfully articulate, persuasively self-confident, frequently unimpressed with corporate rank and organization charts. Also, they often make quick and effective impressions on business leaders who have become impatient and disenchanted with the elaborately statistical and stuffy reports of their regular researchers. The executives may not want to believe the motivation researcher outright, but they admire his dash and sauciness. In private, they confess their admiration by telling each other that 'he certainly has a lot of provocative ideas' or 'you may not always agree with him, but he has more new ideas than anybody who's come down the pike in a long time'. These characteristics of M-R men are admirable and refreshing. They result in quick and effective communication. They add spice to the listening executive's professional life. But the very fact that they communicate more effectively should make executives that much more discriminating in what they believe and accept. It is well to remember that, regardless of the subject, the things which are most easily believed are those which are most fetchingly presented. It is up to management to avoid being easily taken in by the glittering plausibility of a well-turned phrase.

Anxious Experts

Having got the ear of top management, and with vast sums of money riding on the implementation of some of their ideas, motivation research experts are understandably worried about making mistakes. Like the physician who invariably consults his colleagues before settling on a diagnosis in a difficult case, the M-R man consults other M-R men. The form that this consultation takes is often hidden and not even apparent to those who are involved. What might account for this? Let us speculate:

Motivation research is a comparatively new discipline, with many of the practitioners scattered around the country having got their training in the same schools and the same research firms.

Common backgrounds may not automatically lead researchers to produce similar answers to identical questions asked by different companies, but they certainly create a powerful tendency in that direction. The many professional friendships so established in former days continue to lead to a lot of casual shoptalk among people who have since gone their separate ways. This, like the casual exchange of ideas among golfing physicians, is an important kind of professional consultation. It gets more formalized in annual seminars, refresher courses, professional connections, and professional publications.

Out of these continuing close contacts there emerge consensuses about problems, issues, ideas, practices, theories, and so forth. There is always dissent, of course, but there is also always a broad core of agreement.

This kind of agreement is neither intentional nor malicious. It actually rises from the same sort of honest search for truth which in every field of science has always produced widely accepted conventional theories which have later proved false and now seem just plain naïve. Motivation research has had a bitter uphill battle against the closed shop of the so-called 'nose counters'. No wonder it is a tight community of practitioners, even if warring functions erupt occasionally.

But the situation of motivation research differs from the history of many other disciplines in that there is so little experimental verification of its claims and seemingly less inclination to validate them with acceptable statistical tests. I do not say that everything they say or claim must be statistically verified. Far from it. That would reduce researcher experts to mere handymen. What I do say is that compulsively to refuse to attempt statistical verification of their claims, especially where such verification or testing is possible and might be meaningful – to do this is sheer pretentiousness and gross negligence. Yet that refusal is reaching pathological proportions among some motivation researchers. They have even developed a motivation research justification for their refusal.

Tastes or Tests?

Thus Pierre Martineau, one of its most articulate advocates, defends motivation research's introspective, non-statistical preference by declaring, 'Truth is a feeling, not a fact. We "know" that something is true because, inside of us, our feelings "tell" us that it is true.' He argues, 'Insights are furnished by the subconscious mind. But there is no subconscious mind in the IBM machine.'[1]

This is a perfectly legitimate argument for the expert to make. He has a right and duty to speak his mind, to argue a point regarding, say, customer preferences, from his position of recognized scientific expertness in the field. But motivation research is a peculiar 'science'. Its 'experts', like astrologers, are often self-proclaimed rather than publicly acclaimed. Moreover, M-R's situation differs from other 'scientific' disciplines in that its new, and frequently unprovable, ideas are often immediately applied in costly and enormously risky business situations – something that has never been true of raw new ideas in the physical or biological sciences. No wonder motivation researchers seem to feel an urgency about establishing the respectability of both their practices and their ideas.

The easiest road to respectability is to avoid appearances of discord and professional immaturity. Hence on many issues and problems that might ordinarily divide them, there emerges a sort of unintentional and spontaneous agreement – a party line that becomes a protective integument against outside suspicion and criticism. It may be that it is this urgent quest for respectability, rather than the sophisticated scientific maturity of M-R, that accounts for the sameness of the advice that was apparently given to the industries discussed above.

I have investigated this possibility with several well-known M-R practitioners, and they stoutly maintain that no amount of psychological analysis would validate such a hypothesis. They agree, however, that in the case of detergents, for example, even if all aspects of each brand were not thoroughly

[1] Pierre Martineau, *Motivation in Advertising*, McGraw-Hill Book Company, Inc, New York, 1957, pp. 119, 29.

researched before the product was launched, everybody connected with it had already been so completely steeped in psychological approaches to brand and advertising policy that they, in effect, acted as if they were their own motivation researchers. They made their decisions on the basis of the kind of sophisticated 'feel' Pierre Martineau talks about.

Regarding the possibility that agreement may be the result of M-R men having similar professional backgrounds and connections, one nationally known M-R consultant not long ago claimed during a client meeting that the whole premise is wrong – their backgrounds and connections were much too diverse for this to happen. But when the meeting broke up for lunch, virtually the entire luncheon conversation was about the present employment of a large number of M-R alumni of his firm and how well they were doing as M-R professionals.

Sincerest Form of Flattery

Now let us look at the second explanation offered for so much product and advertising similarity – imitation.

Everybody knows there is a lot of conscious imitation in products, packaging, promotion, and TV programming. Examples have already been given. But in the case of liquid cleaners the obvious similarities cannot be due entirely to imitation. Lestoil was the innovator, but the only thing its late-coming competitors imitated was the product itself. Their brand names, their packages, and their promotions were their own. Mr Clean was being market-tested about a year before Handy Andy and Genie appeared. The names, packages, and claims of the latter two may have been deliberate imitations, though this is vigorously denied. And there is no reason to doubt the denials.

If there was any kind of deliberate imitation, it is more likely that it came from an entirely different industry. The psychologist Paul Lazarsfeld has suggested to me that perhaps Marlboro's enormously successful technique of inverting the sex image impressed the soap companies and their agencies. They may be trying to appeal to women, as Marlboro did with both men and women, with a product symbolism of masculine potency. This sort of cross-product copying is fairly common. Thus when the emphasis on youthfulness and modernness succeeds with one product, dozens of different products quickly use the same theme. Lighthearted humour succeeds for beer, and soon it is used for bread, gasoline, and aluminium foil.

But in the present case, while the inversion of the sex symbol is obviously there, how is it that three giant, experienced, ear-to-the-ground companies simultaneously discovered this remote connection and suddenly used precisely the same image for the same product at about the same time? It is too much to expect that it was accident. And as demonstrated by the research on prunes (one of the rare cases where the entire package of a specific client-sponsored motivation research job became publicly available), it is too much to expect that the similarity is due entirely to the sophistication of M-R.

In view of the sequence of events, some sort of imitation cannot be ruled out. These all too similar sales programmes did not spring simultaneously into existence. Mr Clean antedated Handy Andy and Genie. Studebaker's Lark preceded the 'Big Three' by a full year. In menthol cigarettes, Kool had been around a long time. Yet to think that these companies consciously imitated one another is to assume that advertising executives do not realize that identical themes obviously deprive individual brands of profit-building distinctiveness; so it is ridiculous to suppose that very much of what happened was deliberately imitative. But how much of it was unconscious we will never know.

Regardless of how the advertising themes became similar, once they were so obviously and almost humorously alike, why didn't the companies take immediate action? To be sure, the brand names could not be changed, and it would have been unwise to change package designs so soon after launching. But why not change the advertising and the promotions? Why stubbornly violate the rules that sell?

Of course, resisting a developing norm can be costly – as in the early 1950s when Chrysler cars stubbornly stuck with the boxy design, or when some beer companies delayed switching from bottles to cans. But it is one thing to shift gradually into league with a slowly developing and successful trend. It is quite another, as in the case of the three products cited above, for everyone uniformly to adopt the same norm for entirely new products. When this happens, it is time to raise eyebrows.

As I have said, it seems very unlikely that all this similarity was the result of conscious imitation by one company of the brand name, product design, and packaging of its successful competitor. It is ridiculous to suppose that Ford's Falcon consciously imitated the Lark name or that Alpine consciously imitated Kool's colours. Only a company that wanted to make a quick killing would do that – unless it were especially shortsighted. Brand names and package designs are long-term commitments. They represent relatively fixed policies. You rarely change them, and when you do, it is with extreme caution. The images which they are designed to project require a lot of thought regarding their long-run competitive viability. You cannot alter them as easily as Marlboro can gradually remove the tattoo from its he-man heroes.

To the extent that these brand names, brand symbols, and packages were recognized as involving long-term commitments, it seems especially unlikely that the respective companies intentionally froze themselves into a hall-of-mirrors identicalness. Yet in spite of all apparent logic against it, this suicidal commitment has been made repeatedly in recent years. Why this open-eyed, this compulsive, commercial masochism?

Madcap Management

The answer, I think, is that management has failed to manage. It has been seduced not so much by the self-confident and plausible claims of its researchers as by the notion that a properly professional manager must these days rely more on research than on his own wits. But the seduction has not been wholly involuntary. Management has been a compliant victim; at least, it has put up only a token resistance in order to preserve the customary appearance of self-assured virtue.

Management has cooperated in its own seduction because

commercial research seems to promise executive nirvana. If consumer research can reduce uncertainty and risk, there is a strong tendency to believe that it might be able to eliminate them. Its seeming power to liberate the executive from the everyday anxieties of decision making is tantalizing indeed. As a result, more and more executive action is postponed until research has spoken. Instead of facilitating decisions, therefore, research may be contributing to acute managerial indecision. And the feed-back result of the whole process may be that, instead of research making researchers more secure and their output therefore more reliable, their output is actually getting less reliable.

The yield of motivation researchers *seems* increasingly reliable. But is such an appearance based on proof or on posture? Researchers have discovered that the rapid acceptance of their art is not the unmixed blessing they expected. Donald L. Kanter, executive director of the Creative Research Department of Tathem-Laird Advertising, Inc, has exposed this without mercy in his discussion, 'Researchers in Search of a New Image'.[2] M-R people have become understandably worried about the untrustworthy quality of their product, and that is one reason why so many of their studies carry the admonition that 'this is a preliminary report based on early findings'.

Because motivation research is still a comparatively rudimentary art, it is often difficult to get reliable substantiation of its claims. The 'reliability' of some M-R findings becomes lodged not in proof but in the persuasive affirmations of its practitioners, and in the way their presentations carefully appeal to the client's 'feelings' which 'tell' him that it is 'true'. When the research finally says that two man-years of careful study 'suggest' that you need a two-syllable brand name which is familiar to the English vocabulary and which has suggestions of vitality, modernness, youthfulness, strength, lightness, flight, and romantic valour – when it lays this before the auto executive, who is he to fight this prodigious outpouring from

[2] Donald L. Kanter, 'Researchers in Search of a New Image', *Madison Avenue*, August 1959, p. 180.

professional experts all in total agreement? Will he risk every-thing by selecting an unfamiliar or alien name in order to honour himself or a dead relative? The unhappy aftermath of the Edsel, the Tucker, the Frazier, and the Henry J. is too fresh in mind for this kind of self-willed executive action.

If elaborate research tells the executive that green fields and ice-capped coolness will make the customer feel kindly to-wards his product, is he going to defy our current reverence for science by saying, 'That may be okay in theory, but in practice people like pictures of muddy elephants and that's what we're going to give them'?

If an awesome combination of PhD and Phi Beta Kappa talent tells the executive that 'a bald Turkish eunuch, wearing a single earring'[3] and radiating masculine prowess is the proper symbol for an all-purpose liquid detergent, can the executive be blamed for submitting to such well-sponsored and self-assured advice? As Steuart Henderson Britt, himself a PhD and former research executive, has said: 'Some business-men are suckers for buying so-called research because a man is called doctor.'[4] It is perfectly in order for businessmen to 'buy' so-called 'research' or 'expert' advice, but not merely because a man claims expertness. It has to be demonstrated first, otherwise the man is not an expert, no matter how thick his Viennese accent.

Research and Management's Job

Management has often let itself be seduced by the pre-tentious claims of unreliable researchers largely because it does not consider what happens a seduction. Rather, it considers the whole affair highly scientific. And this has been a particularly congenial submission because management has always sought formulas and prescriptions for easier decision making. But calling this science is like confusing a spade with a steam shovel.

[3] This characterization is from 'Guys in Advertising', *The Times Literary Supplement*, special edition on 'The American Imagina-tion', London, November 6th, 1959, p. 34.

[4] *Advertising Age*, February 17th, 1958, p. 68.

One reason management has become particularly suscept-
ible to the seductions of science in recent years is that it has
lost confidence in the legitimacy of its own function. The
remarkable claims, capabilities, and accomplishments of
science are in galloping ascendance. Many executives quake in
the shadow of its complex mechanisms and strident self-
confidence – even those whose own academic training years
ago was in science. By comparison, the practice of management often seems to them a sloppy and slightly second-rate
affair, although they always put on a convincing front of
untroubled self-assurance. When the equally self-assured
motivation researchers tell them exciting tales of research dis-
coveries and policy implications, the insecure decision makers
listen eagerly, even though they may make a token display of
thoughtful scepticism. They should and must listen. And they
have a perfect right to expect their researchers to make the
most of their findings. But management has no right to let
researchers get the upper hand, to accept indiscriminately
what it is told.

If it is any consolation, the business executive should realize
that the highest form of achievement is always art, never
science, and that business leadership *is* an art worthy of his
own respect and the public's plaudits. When easy formulas and
scientific claims are accepted and employed without sufficient
regard for the market conditions under which they will have to
function, the senseless muddle that characterizes liquid
cleaners, compact cars, and mentholated cigarettes is produced. No matter how many carefully controlled laboratory
tests tell you that what is best for menthol cigarettes is green
waterfalls beneath snow-capped mountains, the appropriate
policy may be to *avoid* using these images if everybody else is
using them. In marketing, sound strategy often consists not in
doing a better job of what competitors are doing but in doing
what they are *not* doing.

The more responsible motivation researchers, like Herta
Herzog of McCann-Erickson, Inc, have carefully emphasized
that 'knowledge of motivations does not by itself entail know-

ledge of the best appeals',[5] and that the really effective researcher will act as a diagnostician and definer of the whole market and its problems, not just as a technician antiseptically confining himself to the strict limits of the product or brand he is researching.[6] Knowledge of the consumer's inner needs is not enough. Regardless of the subject, there is no reason to suppose that when we have gained infinite knowledge it will solve all problems. To believe this is to make a fetish of our own illusions.

Let's Motivate Managers

It is the duty of the decision-making executive to use all the consumer research facts that can be made available, but it is his primary duty to use them creatively in combination with all that can be known and predicted about the actual environment of the selling–buying situation.

The important consumer reaction is not what name and colour he prefers when he is quizzed by a researcher in his living room or in an isolation booth, but what name and colour will be *most effective*, given the entire array of names and colours that are encountered in the advertising and point-of-purchase situation.

Motivation research does not and cannot make any outright claim to unimpeachable business virtue. The beguiling influence of research must not be permitted to take its toll in executive indecision and sterile policies. In some fast-moving consumer-goods lines a lot of what is being done seems more rationalized than rational. Management seems to treat certain research findings as monolithic, requiring little of the executive in the way of judgement or of integration with all the other considerations that impinge on the market.

This integrating job is what the compact-car, the cleaner, and the cigarette executives have not done well. Although they obviously know better, some have tended to act as if their respective products are sold in a research vacuum, where it is only necessary to know what is deep down in the psychological

[5] Herta Herzog, *Broadcasting*, February 17th, 1958, p. 90.
[6] Kanter, op. cit., p. 36.

recesses of the consumer's mind. Is it this unequivocal sellout to the fast generalizations of an immature discipline that accounts for the chaotic redundancy about which I have been speaking?

Finally, this lack of integration also accounts for the senseless sameness of so much current 'corporate-image' advertising. While corporate images are important, the faddishness that now encrusts this subject is perhaps worse than not having any clear-cut image at all. Numerous companies that operate or hope to operate within the expanding orbit of electronics and science, for example, have launched corporate-image advertising campaigns. With a few very effective exceptions, the images these ads are projecting look and sound repetitiously alike. All of them emphasize what has already become a commonplace and monotonous theme – scientific prowess which is synthesized in equally commonplace and monotonous pictures of rockets, space stations, electronic controls, atomic structures of matter.

So the advertising pages of leading business magazines often look like a huge, protoplasmic glob of celestial colours and scientific gadgetry. Because of the redundancy of their themes, it is doubtful whether this orgiastic outpouring of corporate narcissism is any more persuasive than a communist agitator at a General Electric stockholders' meeting.

Every effort and every statement addresses itself to a customer. It does not matter whether it comes from a businessman, an artist, a preacher, or a panhandler. If it does not penetrate the curtain of noise and distraction that surrounds the customer, it cannot reach him – no matter how willing the customer is to listen. If the message is not clear, distinctive, meaningful (not just in terms of the customer's personal needs and experiences but also in relation to the competitive messages with which he is bombarded), then the message has not got through. It is management's unique and inescapable duty to see that it does. This requires a consideration not only of the convincing qualities of the message itself but also of the competitive environment within which it must battle for recognition and the customer's patronage.

11

CENTRIPETAL MARKETING

ONE OF the most wasteful features of modern marketing is its fragmenting and centrifugal character – the way a company's efforts will confuse and alienate customers rather than clearly persuade and attract them.

Too often a company will imply one thing about its product in its mass-media ads and contradict it at point of sale, deny it with its direct-selling tactics, and muddle it with its product service policy.

An appliance manufacturer will sponsor expensive TV spectaculars that tell an exotic story of product beauty and functional virtues. But then its dealers will run local ads in which the products are presented as if they were the leftover refuse of a fire sale. At the point of sale the well-dressed, articulate, and reassuring announcer from the TV screen is replaced by a pushy and uninformed salesman in a store the layout and fixtures of which contradict every single impression left by the costly props of the TV commercials. Moreover, the manufacturer's delivery trucks look less like the property of a producer of reliable, modern, electrical equipment than they do like the property of the local Goodwill agency. And the company's letterhead looks less like that of a manufacturer of a modern, reliable piece of complex equipment and more like that of a manufacturer of buggy whips.

In short, the communications job which advertising and good product design so laboriously and expensively undertook is scuttled by the customer's actual experience with the many other communications the company sends out. The overall message that will finally have got through to the customer will be self-contradictory and confusing instead of self-reinforcing and reassuring.

The average consumer is assaulted by about fifteen hundred

commercial messages daily – on TV, radio, billboards, brand labels on ketchup bottles, cars, pencils, and so forth. A massive din of commercial noise inundates every customer, whether a housewife, a purchasing agent, or a design engineer.

This means that more than ever the business firm has to be systematically self-conscious about every commercial message it sends out – whether it concerns its ads, its product design, its packages, its letterhead, how its salesmen dress and what they say, its point-of-sale materials, its trucks, or the conditions under which its products are displayed and sold.

It is essential that the messages of each of these be carefully coordinated to achieve one overwhelming, self-reinforcing, simple, and persuasive story. Otherwise the company won't penetrate the colossal curtain of noise that shrouds the consumer. The more fragmenting, self-contradictory, and discordant these messages are, the more likely the customer will become confused, unconvinced, and irritated. He'll just shut off his hearing aid. The more self-reinforcing, consistent, and unifying the messages are, the more likely they'll penetrate the noise curtain and produce sales.

In short, everything a company does – in marketing and everything else – has to be unifying and centripetal, not fragmenting and centrifugal. This requires total overall corporate planning and coordination. To assume that only marketing addresses the customer is a mistake – a mistake that can cost dearly. And that is why the effective modern corporation needs a constant top-down look at its total communications consequences, so that the total communications programme is always designed for maximum customer penetration.

The Case of the Centrifugal Treasurer

Suppose, as a corporation president, you had been trying unsuccessfully for months to find a new treasurer for your company. Finally you received a promising letter in answer to an ad. The letter was well written on quality personal stationery, and the man's qualifications looked exceedingly interesting. But there were a couple of smudged finger marks on the letter.

You invite the man to an interview at your home at two o'clock on a Sunday afternoon. He comes precisely on time, pulling up on an extremely loud motorcycle, with bushy red foxtails trailing from the handlebars. He is well dressed in a well-pressed conservative business suit, though you notice his fingernails need cleaning. He has a pleasant manner and clearly knows corporate accounting and finance. While he communicates with ease, contrary to his letter his grammar is sometimes poor. He obviously knows your business and has some good ideas on the financial management of your company. He seems particularly knowledgeable on the costs and advantages of different ways of handling the company's long-term capital needs. After he has sketched out a few examples of the relative costs of several financing alternatives, you notice that he made a minor error in addition.

Now, if at this point you had to tell the man that you were either interested in him or not, what would you do?

First of all, you would probably argue that the above illustration is simply 'too far out' to take seriously. A man applying for an important job such as treasurer simply would not behave this way. That is true – to sell himself he wouldn't. But the sad fact is that to sell their products a great many companies behave precisely this way. The very executives who would never behave as the treasurer did when it comes to their personal affairs behave exactly as he did when it comes to the products they sell.

Let us look more carefully at what the treasurer did. His original letter was very impressive (we might call this the 'copy of his ad'); it came on fine stationery (we could call this 'the magazine in which his ad appeared'); but there were smudged spots on the letter ('poor layout'). The man ('the product') arrived in a fine suit ('package'), although the motorcycle ('delivery truck') raised a lot of questions as to 'what kind of a character is this'.

The product seemed to have both the versatility and the special uses required, although it made a strange noise ('poor grammar'); and in one application the reliability was off just a little ('error in addition'). Still the product fitted into your setup, was easily available, and its ads cited a successful history of wide usage – although you wondered a little how it could really have had a thoroughly successful history in view of the fact that dirt tended to accumulate in one of its strategic operating parts (the fingernails).

Should you buy the product? Would you have any interest in this man? Probably not, you feel. There are too many contradictions. The overall impression doesn't hang together in a convincing manner. It has a centrifugal quality, telling different and contradictory stories about the product instead of one, single, self-reinforcing tale.

The man's letter, dress, and ideas tell you one thing about him. But his motorcycle contradicts his dress; his addition, his ideas; and his grammar, his letter. In short, there is a centrifugal or fragmenting quality to the impression he creates.

If he had come on a more powerful motorcycle, if he had done his additions in blue ink instead of ordinary pencil, and if he had spoken in a deeper and more authoritative voice, would your opinion of him be any better? No. The contradictions about him would simply have become more obvious. Your reservations would be strengthened.

Why 'Marketing Costs Too Much'

But the executive who refuses to hire the prospect who projects such a centrifugal impression of himself often spends vast amounts of money to produce the same kinds of enormously centrifugal and fragmenting messages in 'support' of the product that his own company is trying to sell.

No wonder sales aren't so hot. He himself just refused to buy a 'product' that told conflicting things about itself, so why should other people buy *his* product when it is equally contradictory?

No wonder this executive feels that 'marketing costs too much', that 'we're getting less sales bang for the buck'.

The reason so many companies these days are not getting enough sales bang for their bucks is not because they are not spending enough bucks, and not even necessarily because they are spending them the wrong way. The reason is frequently that they are not spending them in a *consistent* way. They are trying to build sales by saying too many different things and in too many different ways.

Thus a meat-packer's TV ads give the impression that the company is friendly and neighbourly; its radio ads, young and aggressive; its magazine ads, sophisticated and smart; its delivery trucks, tough and solid; its letterhead, old and conservative; but the package in which its frankfurters are wrapped (the thing its ads talked about and in regard to which the customer has to choose) – the package looks as if its contents might be as transparently thin (and therefore lacking in solid nourishment) as the package itself is transparent and flimsy.

In order to get more sales bang for its buck, what should the company do? Spend even more? Get itself a more imaginative advertising agency? Have more point-of-sale promotions? Distribute coupons and samples? In short, is the company's solution to become a more creative or a smarter outfit?

No. The problem is not to be more creative. The problem is to be *less* centrifugal.

The problem with the meat-packer is that it has confused the public by showing a lot of contradictory pictures of itself. To spend more money, to think up newly creative approaches – these just compound the confusion. The trouble with this company is that its sales messages (whether on radio or TV, in magazines, on its trucks, logotype, letterhead, or packages) – its many messages are as competitive with each other as they are numerous. Instead of each of these messages reinforcing the others, and therefore giving the customer a clear, exact idea of what the company and its product do – instead of this, each message might as well be from a different company trying to tell a different story with different and conflicting claims. The combined effort is centrifugal, tearing the company's total message apart into a lot of competing and contradictory fragments.

The Forgotten Customer

This kind of centrifugal, costly, customer-confusing activity can take many forms. Take the case of a bank's trying to expand the range of its services to individuals and small businesses. The Chase Manhattan Bank of New York tries to do this through a heavily supported television advertising campaign based on the theme that 'you have a friend at the Chase Manhattan'. It tells people in all walks of life of the many things, personal and business, which the bank is eager to do for them. It advises them to come into the bank any time. The ads are well done, and the advice and help given to customers are thoroughly useful.

But the programme lacks a crucial ingredient. It has forgotten to look at the potential customer's total and highly personal problem when he thinks of banks. Let us say an ordinary wage earner or small businessman or housewife is thinking about taking up the Chase Manhattan's offer.

The first thing that will come to that person's mind is a picture of how the insides of banks usually look – big, spacious, strong, businesslike, and austere. Immediately doubts spring into his mind. Do those ads really mean it? Are they talking about me when they say 'You have a friend . . .' – Or are they talking to a college graduate who takes winter vacations in Bermuda? Even if I went there, whom would I see? Whom would I ask for directions? The guard? The teller? An information girl? What will I ask for? Do I have to explain my whole problem to one of *these* people? Such questions are enough to keep people away.

In other words, when it gets right down to the crucial entity – the customer – Chase's programme has not been planned as thoroughly as the needs of the customer require. Indeed, the ads may create negative reactions among a sizeable group of people they are addressing. The programme is centrifugal.

To get the customer to deal with you requires more than simply developing a service or a product the customer needs and then telling him about it. At the outset it requires a carefully planned and fully integrated programme – a complete package. In the case of Chase Manhattan, a more self-conscious concern for the customer, regarding all aspects of his thinking, his station in life, and how these relate to the kind of establishment a bank is – these considerations would have resulted in one more step than was actually taken. The ads would have told the TV viewer to come to a special counter in each Chase bank which would be prominently marked, say, 'Service Secretary'. The ads would announce that in each bank this person is especially trained and assigned to receive all new inquiries and service calls and that all a customer need to do is briefly explain his or her problem and he will be directed to a helpful bank official who deals with such problems regularly and confidentially. People could also call by telephone and ask for the Service Secretary.

The Service Secretary would have other responsibilities too, such as perhaps doing routine typing for the various bank departments. But for the self-doubting customer who is thinking about seeing his 'friend at the Chase', the announced availability of the Service Secretary would eliminate the present worries about whom to see, how to ask, and whether the ads are really inviting everybody. It would stop the kinds of self-doubting questions which ordinarily would keep the customer from taking up the bank's offer.

The result of this addition to Chase's programme would convert it from being self-defeating and 'centrifugal' into being self-reinforcing and 'centripetal'.

Getting and Keeping Customers

As we have said before, the first business of every business is to stay in business. To do that you have to get and keep customers, and you have to do so in a ruthless marketplace.

No responsible executive these days needs to be told that it takes more than a 'better mousetrap' for people to beat a path to his door. In fact, the better-mousetrap theory of getting and keeping customers has never under any circumstances been anything more than a naïve half-truth.

Everybody who wasn't born yesterday knows that you first have to get people to know and believe in your product or service enough to make them actively dissatisfied with the fact that they don't have it. You have to get the product to them, and where, when, and in the manner that they want it. That is why we have advertising, sales promotion, salesmen, industrial designers, warehouses, wholesalers, retail stores, and expense accounts. And all these are costly.

In fact, the most common complaint you hear these days is that 'marketing costs too much'. We are getting less sales bang for the buck. Hence there is a frantic search among marketing executives for new and novel sales-building devices – magic shortcuts to doubtful success. The result is that the market is flooded with an avalanche of vulgar sales gimmicks such as wild consumer contests, useless giveaways, and sales meetings on ocean liners headed for San Juan. There is a ceaseless outpouring of tasteless, meaningless, and silly advertising. And there are a lot of enormously expensive company reorganizations.

The result of all this wits-end activity is that its perpetrator often gets an even less solid bang for his buck. The reason is obvious enough. The pushy multiplicity of sales messages that now assault the ears and eyes of the customer makes him confused, irritated, distracted, sceptical, or just plain fed up. The din is so great that he simply shuts off his hearing aid.

He may not do it in any self-consciously deliberate way, but he does it in fact. He hears less, he believes less, he buys less. This is his unconscious way of fighting back.

But even companies that have kept their heads and refused to make obscene spectacles of themselves by pulling out all stops – even these companies often commit the same errors as their brethren, except they are less noisy about it. Our modest meat-packer is a good example.

To get and keep customers means that you must, among other things, communicate properly with them. But this obviously involves a lot more:

1. What to communicate – not just what your product or service is, but what it means to the customer. ('Don't sell the steak, sell the sizzle')

2. When to communicate – not just in actual sales, or 'advertising' situations, but perhaps when the prospect is least aware of being addressed

3. How to communicate – not just via the conventional

media, but also via the design of the product, its package, its brand name and how it looks, the delivery truck the product comes in, the letterhead on which you write the customer, the outside appearance of your factories, and many other things

It is obvious that there are dozens of ways a company communicates with the public, dozens of ways it tells something about itself to the customer. Yet it is essential to recognize that every company faces stiff competition from companies far outside its own industry. Everybody is your competitor in some way because thousands of different companies are trying daily to tell your prospective customer something about themselves, trying to get him to buy their particular goods or services. Everybody competes for his attention, his patronage, his scarce money.

It therefore stands to reason that every time you address the customer you should avoid the fragmenting centrifugal practices of the meat-packer and the job hunter. In order to outdo the thousands of competitive communications that assault the customer daily, each of your many messages must be self-reinforcing and centripetal, not fragmenting and centrifugal.

This has been proved by eminent psychologists in clinical investigations and by studies of the relative effectiveness of centrifugal versus centripetal business communication.

As the result there has been a growing interest in recent years in the field of 'corporate identity'. This is the effort to make every communication of a business firm give an identical, carefully predetermined impression of the company and its products. Popularly this is referred to as projecting the desired 'company image'. In its vastness this idea results in carefully planning the nature and technique of every way in which the firm communicates to the public – packages; product design; store, factory, office, waiting-room, and warehouse design; product and brand name selection; letterhead, logo, and calling-card design; advertising; point-of-purchase materials; public relations activities; and marketing strategy and tactics.

All this is now widely considered an important part of the total strategy of getting and keeping customers – of getting more sales bang from the buck in the increasingly more competitive marketplace.

The concept or philosophy underlying 'corporate identity' says, in effect, that the business firm must present a face of consistent and organic wholeness to the public that it addresses. Otherwise it dilutes its effectiveness. As the result it must treat all its communications, including the design of every package, office front, letterhead, product, advertisement, and so forth, as a single integrated effort. It must treat the product, package design, advertising, marketing, and all the supporting consumer research not as separate or separable categories but as an integrated organic whole.

Integrated Communications

No meat-packer would be so resolutely self-assured that he would not first try to find out which of several different kinds of sausage the customer prefers before plunging into the production of a new line of sausages. Yet the same meat-packer will often put this well-researched sausage into almost any kind of package, so long as it meets his particular personal standard of what looks right. He will do almost any kind of advertising. He will do almost any kind of point-of-sale promotion. And he will do all these things differently, in large part because he does not see properly the connection between each. Indeed, his company is often organized along lines that make each of these areas the responsibility of different people. Where the company is organized more sensibly along 'product manager' or 'brand manager' lines, this danger is greatly reduced, but it is frequently far from eliminated. The organization is right, but the marketing theory is wrong.

When our meat-packer hero accepts almost any kind of package design, he knows, of course, that he is not an artist or an expert; but he knows what he likes, and he thinks his tastes are pretty average – like 'the man in the street'. So he becomes his own package designer.

But suppose his competitors have sought out experienced experts to design their sausage package, and the experts themselves have had the advice of experienced consumer researchers – both in helping them to decide in the first place what major sales-building features should characterize the package and later in helping them decide which of several alternative packages with these features the customer would be most likely to buy.

But before putting pencil to paper, suppose the competitor's designer will also consult with marketing experts. The latter will in the meanwhile have studied the product, the special retail conditions under which it is to be sold, the attitudes and problems of the trade, the typical advertising and promotions which competitors use to support the product, the way in which it is prepared and used in the home, and the way in which consumer decisions are made regarding buying the product – that is, is it planned purchase, an impulse purchase, a purchase decided by the buyer or by her children, etc.?

Then all three experts – designer, researcher, and marketer, each perhaps represented by two persons with wide experience in many different product lines – then all six compare notes in a wide-open atmosphere of freewheeling thought in which they develop, sift, and evaluate ideas. Such an 'exchange' or 'planning' session might run several hours or all day. It might finally break up with an agreement that more study or thought of some kind is required before another exchange or planning session can really be fruitful. With the various parties clear on what more is required of them, a new session date will be set.

After this second session the package designer goes to work. He will know exactly the competitive context within which the sausage package must function, he will know who the prospective customer is and what appeals to her, how the competition is operating, what the typical store manager's problems and needs are (for example, would he give more shelf space to a solid square package than to a transparent triangular one?), and what the overall marketing and communications theme of the new product will be and the role packaging will perform in this theme.

In the end the competitive meat-packer will have paid more to get his 'package' design than our hero who did it himself, but there are two important offsetting differences:

1. The 'package' our competitor got was not simply a package within which the sausage was to be wrapped. He will have got a 'total marketing package', which, in effect, helped design the entire product programme.

2. The 'total marketing package' he got would probably more than pay for itself in extra sales during the first six months after the product was launched. After that, the professionally designed package would be like a perpetual-motion machine, constantly turning out incremental revenue without any further cost.

In the end, then, the first meat-packer might have got into the market faster – and spent less to get there – but he might have got infinitely less sales bang for his buck. But as his sales refused to materialize as much as was hoped, he would probably have tried to make things right by pulling out all the promotional stops. This would have diluted his corporate or product 'image' even more, confused the customer more, and merely reduced further the return per dollar of sales effort.

Customer-oriented Solutions

The first business of every business is to get and keep customers. Even if we concede that, all other things being equal, a better mousetrap will attract more customers than a worse one, the question remains this: What is better? Who decides, the engineer who invented it, the company president who authorized the money for it, the copywriter who did the advertising, or the customer? But how does the customer decide? Are his standards the same as the engineer? Will he believe the advertising copywriter?

Obviously, the needs, attitudes, and problems of the customer are crucial – in everything.

For example, a leading firm of industrial designers was recently asked to redesign the main restaurant in a famous old hotel. The restaurant's business was poor and getting worse. The client wanted it 'modernized'.

After careful study of the situation, the men in the design firm who were assigned to the project held the kind of exchange or planning session described above. The research representative in the session pointed out that all the other top restaurants in town had a 'modern' decor while the hotel's major restaurant was nineteenth-century Victorian with vast ceilings, elaborate sculpturing, and huge glass chandeliers. The hotel itself was built along the same motif. Yet only a fraction of the people who stayed at the hotel ate there. They went to the modern places. Further research indicated that people of means in the community – and many middle-class people who celebrated anniversaries and other occasions by eating out – that while these people liked the new modern restaurants, they did not feel that they were anything really 'special' or unique. They lacked the exclusivity and sumptuousness which the 'occasions' demanded, or the pocketbooks allowed, or tastes preferred.

The planning session concluded that, instead of modernizing the hotel's main dining room, it should be restored. It should be turned into a palace of sumptuousness and aristocratic elegance. It should resurrect the older virtues of quiet dignity and of pride in custom-made quality. The spacious ceilings should be emphasized, not boarded up and hidden. The ornate sculpturing should be repainted and spotlighted, not ripped down and replaced by a modern abstract design. The chandeliers should be cleaned and brightened, not traded in for recessed fluorescent.

In short, the design firm made a complete market analysis before putting pencil to drawing board. As the result, instead of proposing an even better modern decor than that of the city's other restaurants, it proposed going counter to the prevailing trend. Instead of making the dining room modern – instead of doing a better job of what competitors were already doing well – it suggested doing what they were not doing.

The client reacted about as was expected – violently against it. He said that he had made up his mind, had told the designers what he wanted, and that, if they did not care to supply what he was willing to pay for, he would get himself other designers.

The design firm persisted, showing him the evidence of its consumer research, its marketing analysis, its estimate of market potentials, and its design rationale. It showed him in sketches what could be done. It also said that with the restoration of the idea of dignified sumptuousness and aristocratic excellence in decor, the same motif would have to be carried through in every other aspect of the redesigned dining room's operation. Therefore the firm would design menu covers, waiter uniforms, table linens; select the china, glassware and sterling flatware; and, with the cooperation of a leading New York chef, make menu recommendations.

After much argument and delay, the client finally agreed to the suggested proposal. Today the restaurant is the most thriving in the city. It automatically comes to mind when people in the city think of celebrating an important occasion by eating out. Anybody who wants to impress a guest with genuine sumptuousness and dignified quality always takes him to 'The Centennial Room' – the new name especially selected by the design firm.

All this shows how genuinely creative and profitable a truly customer-oriented communications programme can be. It has to be animated by the only approach that really makes sense in this competitive world – the theory of 'centripetal marketing'. In the restaurant redesign, every message that was 'sent out' was self-reinforcing. Every message was based on a thorough study of the customer, the competition, the historic position of the communicator in his community. It left no relevant stone unturned. When the curtain was finally lifted and the product launched, there was no doubt about what the product communicated, no ambiguity or contradiction in what it said about itself. The sales bang for the buck was enormous.

To get and keep customers requires that you understand them, that everything you do be part of an integrated, centripetal communications, marketing, and product effort. As the competition for the customer's attention and dollar gets more fierce, it becomes an increasingly wasteful (and perhaps fatal) luxury for the business firm to treat the various aspects of its product, communications, and marketing policies as somehow separate and discrete pigeonhole parts. No company can afford not to use the more encompassing, consolidating, customer-getting concept of centripetal marketing. And it cannot afford to avoid or constantly postpone developing a clear statement of its goals and directions, otherwise it may wastefully practise centripetal marketing on the wrong products at the wrong time and with the wrong results.

INDEX

MANAGEMENT AND MARKETING SERIES

Mathematics
for the Million 10/6

LANCELOT HOGBEN

'a book of first class importance...should be read by every intelligent youth from 15 to 90, who is trying to get the hang of things in this universe.' H. G. WELLS

'If only I had been brought up on this book, the *sense* and meaning of mathematics would have been made clear to me' A. L ROWSE

'He deals with maths in a way that they never taught us at school...' DAILY EXPRESS

The Trachtenberg
Speed System of
Basic Mathematics 5/-

Translated and adapted by
ANN CUTLER and RUDOLPH McSHANE

'His teaching is brilliant' GUARDIAN

'Diligently studied for, say one month, it will enable any normal adult to become a highly skilled, fast and accurate calculator.'
HIGHER EDUCATION JOURNAL

A SELECTION OF POPULAR READING IN PAN

☐ PRIDE AND PREJUDICE Jane Austen		3/6
☐ INHERITANCE Phyllis Bentley		7/6
☐ SHOOTING SCRIPT Gavin Lyall		5/-
☐ WUTHERING HEIGHTS Emily Brontë		3/6
☐ HONEYBUZZARD Angela Carter		3/6
☐ ALONG THE CLIPPER WAY		
	Sir Francis Chichester (illus.)	6/-
☐ ROSEMARY'S BABY Ira Levin		5/-
☐ EAGLE DAY Richard Collier (illus.)		6/-
☐ THE MAN WITH THE GOLDEN GUN Ian Fleming		3/6
☐ THE SPY WHO LOVED ME Ian Fleming		3/6
☐ THE MAGUS John Fowles		8/6
☐ THE CASE OF THE WAYLAID WOLF		
	Erle Stanley Gardner	3/6
☐ I CAN SEE YOU BUT YOU CAN'T SEE ME		
	Eugene George	5/-
☐ THE ROOM UPSTAIRS Monica Dickens		5/-
☐ A SENTENCE OF LIFE Julian Gloag		6/-
☐ SISTERS UNDER THEIR SKINS Jane Grant		3/6
☐ FAR FROM THE MADDING CROWD		
	Thomas Hardy	5/-
☐ THE RELUCTANT WIDOW Georgette Heyer		5/-
☐ FREDERICA Georgette Heyer		5/-
☐ STRANGERS ON A TRAIN Patricia Highsmith		5/-
☐ STORIES MY MOTHER NEVER TOLD ME (Part I)		
	Alfred Hitchcock	3/6
☐ YOUNG BESS Margaret Irwin		5/-
☐ THE DEEP BLUE GOOD-BYE John D. MacDonald		3/6
☐ THE LIFE OF IAN FLEMING		
	John Pearson (illus.)	7/6
☐ SHAMELADY James Mayo		3/6
☐ MADONNA OF THE SEVEN HILLS Jean Plaidy		5/-
☐ SO DISDAINED Nevil Shute		3/6
☐ DIPLOMATIC COVER Dominic Torr		5/-

Obtainable from all booksellers and newsagents. If you
have any difficulty, please send purchase price plus 6d.
postage to PO Box 11, Falmouth, Cornwall.

I enclose a cheque/postal order for selected titles ticked
above plus 6d. per book to cover packing and postage.

NAME ....

ADDRESS ....

....